HORIZON

AUTUMN, 1970 · VOLUME XII, NUMBER 4

Some Words for the Young

Lewis Mumford

Those members of the younger generation who are turned off by the Technocracy, the power structure, the military-industrial complex, and the whole benighted Establishment will find a fellow spirit in Lewis Mumford. For Mr. Mumford has been warning, since long before they were born, that the modern Western "megamachine" is headed for catastrophe. His new book *The Pentagon of Power,* which we present in this issue, is the fruit of a lifetime's thought by one of the most perceptive and original minds of our century. It deserves the attention of all those who care about the course of our civilization. And the new fact is that it will get that attention because Mr. Mumford is no longer a voice crying in the wilderness. His prophecies have come true with such a vengeance that at last he is being listened to.

The disaffected young will be glad to hear that the moral foundations of the "megamachine" have been eroded to such an extent that "a nuclear Ragnarok, or Twilight of the Gods, long ago predicted in Norse mythology," may be in store for the Pentagon of Power. But the young will be wrong if they find in Mumford's book any comfort for those nihilists who turn their backs on reason, reject the lessons of history, and amuse themselves with mindless sensations while waiting for the collapse of Western civilization. Listen to what he has to say:

"More alert in their responses than the older generation to what is going on before their eyes, an active minority among the young are behaving as if a nuclear catastrophe had already in fact occurred. In their minds they are now living among the ruins, without any permanent shelter, without any regular supply of food, without any customs or habits except those they improvise from day to day, without books, without academic credentials, without any fixed vocation or career, without any source of knowledge except the inexperience of their own peers. The revolt is not merely against their elders; it has become, in fact, a revolt against all historic culture—not merely against an overpowered technology and an overspecialized, misapplied intelligence, but against any higher manifestations of the mind.

"In their unconscious, the young are living in a post-catastrophic world; and their conduct would be rational in terms of that world. Only by massing together and touching each other's bodies do they have any sense of security and continuity. So, many of them escape to the open country, form temporary pads, communes, and encampments, anesthetize themselves to cold, rain, mud, hardship, and repulsive sanitary conditions, accept poverty and depri-

AMERICAN HERITAGE PUBLISHING CO.

PRESIDENT
James Parton

EDITORIAL COMMITTEE
Joseph J. Thorndike, *Chairman*
Oliver Jensen
Richard M. Ketchum

SENIOR ART DIRECTOR
Murray Belsky

SENIOR EDITOR, HORIZON
Marshall B. Davidson

PUBLISHER, HORIZON
Paul Gottlieb

EDITOR
Joseph J. Thorndike
MANAGING EDITOR: Charles L. Mee, Jr.
ART EDITOR: Jane Wilson
ART DIRECTOR: Kenneth Munowitz
ASSOCIATE EDITOR: Shirley Tomkievicz
CONTRIBUTING EDITORS: Walter Karp, Barbara Klaw
ASSISTANT EDITORS: David Lloyd-Jones, Mary Sherman Parsons
EDITORIAL ASSISTANT: Michael E. DuBois
COPY EDITOR: Mary Ann Pfeiffer   *Assistant:* Kaethe Ellis
ADVISORY BOARD: Gilbert Highet, *Chairman,* Frederick Burkhardt,
William Harlan Hale, John Walker
EUROPEAN CONSULTING EDITOR: J. H. Plumb, *Christ's College, Cambridge*
EUROPEAN BUREAU: Gertrudis Feliu, *Chief, 11 rue du Bouloi, Paris 1er*

HORIZON

A Magazine of the Arts

AUTUMN, 1970 · VOLUME XII, NUMBER 4

vation; but in compensation, they recover an elemental animal faith, perform acts of mutual aid, hospitality, and love, share freely whatever food or drink they can get hold of, and get pleasure out of each other's physical presence—and out of the reduction of life to the most elemental bodily expressions.

"Since the ruins are still imaginary, these would-be dropouts draw upon the very order they reject. They assemble by motorcar in the tens of thousands to attend their collective 'rock' festivals, actively participating in radio and television happenings, and stone their minds with drugs and druglike music electrically amplified. In short, despite their gestures of revolt against the established goods of civilization, the young are in fact addicted to its most decadent mass products. This is a purely megatechnic primitivism. By reducing their world to a series of addled happenings, they invite the ultimate happening against which they supposedly protest."

The young have as much to learn from Lewis Mumford's wisdom as their elders have. He represents a native intellectual tradition that comes down from Emerson and Thoreau, Melville and Whitman, and a good many other Americans whose voices were drowned out for a while by the clang of nineteenth-century industrial power. They have as much to say to American youth as Indian mystics have, and a lot more than European anarchists.   J.J.T.

HORIZON is published every three months by American Heritage Publishing Co., Inc. Editorial and executive offices: 551 Fifth Avenue, New York, N.Y. 10017. Treasurer: George W. Breitkreuz. Secretary: John C. Taylor 3rd. All correspondence about subscriptions should be addressed to: HORIZON Subscription Office, 379 West Center St., Marion, Ohio 43302.

Single Copies: $6.00. Subscriptions: $20.00 per year in the U.S. & Canada; elsewhere, $21.00

Cumulative indexes for Volumes I–V and VI–X are available at $3. HORIZON is also indexed in the *Readers' Guide to Periodical Literature.* The editors welcome contributions but can assume no responsibility for unsolicited material. Title registered U.S. Patent Office. Second class postage paid at New York, N.Y., and at additional mailing offices.

Ideas

Archaeology

Art and Architecture

History

Letters

Biography

Music

MUSÉE DES TAPISSERIES, ANGERS; LUC JOUBERT

COVER: A seven-headed beast "like unto a leopard" appears in a detail from the Angers Apocalypse tapestry seen above. Illustrating scenes from the Book of Revelation, these great tapestries were begun in 1376 for Louis, Duke of Anjou. The Duke and his royal brothers formed a remarkable quartet of art patrons whose story is told beginning on page 54.

THE PENTAGON OF POWER

The technological "megastructure" that man has built during the last four centuries is faced with erosion of its base in the human will. So says Lewis Mumford, who here examines the forces that may bring it down and the new "organic" society that must replace it

The Paradox of Automation

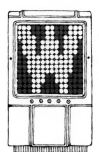

e face now the great paradox of automation, put once and for all in Goethe's fable of the Sorcerer's Apprentice. Our civilization has found a magic formula for setting industrial and academic brooms and pails of water to work by themselves, in ever increasing quantities at an ever increasing speed. But we have lost the Master Magician's spell for altering the tempo

of this process or halting it when it ceases to serve human functions and purposes, though this formula (foresight and feedback) is written plainly on every organic process.

As a result we are already, like the apprentice, beginning to drown in the flood. The moral should be plain: unless one has the power to stop an automatic process—and if necessary reverse it—one had better not start it.

Lewis Mumford has devoted a lifetime to the study of man and the technical civilization he has built. The article that begins on this page is drawn from his new book *The Pentagon of Power*, the second and concluding volume of *The Myth of the Machine,* the first volume of which was published in 1967. *The Pentagon of Power* will be published next year by Harcourt Brace Jovanovich.

To spare ourselves humiliation over our failure to control automation, many of us now pretend that the process conforms exactly to our purposes and alone meets all our needs—or to speak more accurately, we cast away those qualifying human traits that would impede the process. And as our knowledge of isolatable segments and fragments becomes infinitely refined and microscopic, our ability to interrelate the parts and to bring them to a focus in rational activities continues to disappear.

How deeply ingrained the commitment to automatism has become appears from a sad little tale passed on to me by Dennis Gabor, sometime professor of engineering at the Imperial College of Technology in London, himself an adept in some of the most advanced branches of science-oriented technology.

"I do not think that I have told you

about a great hope which I had three years ago. I heard that IBM-France had made a remarkable experiment. In their great factory at Corbeil-Essonnes they made a break with division of labor. One technician completed a sizable element of a computer, using hundreds of tools, tested it himself, and *signed it*, like an artist! I heard also that the gain in interest and the development in intelligence of these workmen was fabulous. Thereupon I wrote an enthusiastic letter to IBM-France and asked to visit them. I got a crestfallen letter, that 'until now it was indeed like this—but their new factory will be fully automated!' " IBM was plainly not concerned with increasing *human* intelligence or giving back to machine workers the quality of life that once was fostered by the higher crafts.

By its own logic automation is dedicated to the installation of a system of total control over every natural process, and ultimately over every organic function and human purpose.

But at this terminal point, where the automatic process is on the verge of creating a whole race of acquiescent and obedient human automatons, the forces of life have begun, sometimes stealthily, sometimes ostentatiously, to reassert themselves in the only form that is left to them: an explosive affirmation of the primal energies of the organism. Already we are faced with a reaction from civilization more desperate than any hitherto visible on the historic record—partly a withdrawal to some bucolic or pastoral simplicity, but even more to a state anterior to the most primitive human institutions, that which Shakespeare characterized as Caliban, and Freud as the primal underlayer of the human personality, the id.

For mark this: the automaton was not born alone. The automaton has been accompanied, we can now see, by a twin, a dark shadow-self: defiant, not docile; disorderly, not organized or controlled; above all, aggressively destructive, even homicidal, reasserting

the dammed-up forces of life in crazy or criminal acts. In the emerging figure of man the subego, or id, threatens to function as the superego in a reversed hierarchy that lowers the authority of the brain and puts the reflexes and blind instincts in command. The aim of this subversive superego is to destroy those higher attributes of man whose gifts of love, mutuality, rationality, imagination, and constructive aptitude have enlarged all the possibilities of life. It is in the light of these impending negations and destructions that the whole concept of subjugating nature and replacing man's own functions with collectively fabricated, automatically programmed and operated, mechanical and electronic equivalents must at last be reappraised.

The
New
Vision

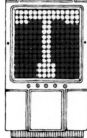

he period that opened in the final years of the fifteenth century has been designated the Age of Exploration, and that characterization covers a good many of the events that followed. But the most significant part of this new exploration took place in the mind; and what is more, the cultural New World that was opened was still attached in fact, even in the Western Hemisphere, to many obscure ramifying roots in the Old World, roots that pushed through heavy layers of soil into the debris of ancient cities and empires.

What was truly new for Western man was the exhilarating sense that, for the first time, every part of the planet was accessible and offered opportunities for daring adventure, for active eco-

nomic intercourse, and even, at least to more reflective minds, for self-enlightenment. Both the earth and the skies lay open to systematic investigation as never before. If the bright starry heavens invited exploration, so did the dark continents across the seas; and so, eventually, did the still darker continent that made up man's cultural and biological past.

Broadly speaking, then, two complementary kinds of exploration beckoned Western man. While they were closely related in their point of origin, they moved in different directions, pursued different goals—though often crossing—and at last merged into a single movement, which increasingly sought to replace the gifts of nature with those more limited fabrications of man that were drawn from a single aspect of nature: that which could be brought under human domination. One exploration focused mainly on the sky and on the orderly motions of planets and falling bodies, on space-measuring and timekeeping, on repetitive events and determinable laws. The other boldly traversed the seas and even burrowed below the surface of the earth, seeking the Promised Land, lured partly by curiosity and cupidity, partly by the desire to break loose from ancient ties and limits.

Between the fifteenth and the nineteenth century the New World opened by the terrestrial explorers, adventurers, soldiers, and administrators joined forces with the scientific and technical new world that the scientists, inventors, and engineers explored and cultivated —they were part and parcel of the same movement. One mode of exploration was concerned with abstract symbols, rational systems, universal laws, repeatable and predictable events, objective mathematical measurements; it sought to understand, utilize, and control the forces that derive ultimately from the cosmos and the solar system. The other mode dwelt on the concrete and the organic, the adventurous, the tangible: to sail uncharted oceans, to conquer new lands, to subdue and overawe strange peoples, to discover new foods and medicines, perhaps to find the Fountain of Youth, or if not that, to seize by shameless force of arms the wealth of the Indies. In both modes of exploration there was from the beginning a touch of defiant pride and demonic frenzy.

Moved by this New World vision, audacious sailing ships breached the geographic barriers that had too long kept the peoples of the earth apart; through these openings during the next few centuries the first trickle of explorers turned into a torrent of emigrants who poured into the Americas, into Australia and New Zealand, into Africa, to seize and settle in their own style great areas of the earth whose indigenous inhabitants had hitherto led a relatively self-centered life.

From the outset, in the sixteenth century, the leaders of European society fervently believed that a great cyclic change in the life of man was about to take place. Poliziano, the imaginative Florentine humanist, promptly declared that the discovery of the New World by Columbus would bring about a beneficent change in human existence; while only a century later the Calabrian monk Campanella, excited by Bacon and Galileo, hopefully hailed with equal fervor the new world of astronomy, physics, and technology, embracing in fantasy the still nameless mechanical and electronic inventions that were bound, he felt sure, to transform human society. After outlining the main features of his ideal commonwealth in *The City of the Sun,* Campanella observed that according to contemporary astrologers the coming age would have more history within a hundred years "than all the world had had in the four thousand years before."

Granted a little charitable latitude, that prophecy proved remarkably correct: the wildest imaginary inventions fell far short of the actual achievements that came to pass within a few centuries. From the beginning this subjective faith in a New World that would transcend all past human achievements took hold of the most sober minds; it had the same effect upon Western man as the flinging back of shutters and the opening of windows in an ancient house that has been sealed up for many winters and has fallen into disrepair. Those who breathed the fresh air of spring were not content to live longer amid the moldy rafters and the cobwebs, even when the heirlooms in their ancient quarters were still serviceable and beautiful. Though they might have hesitated at first to demolish the entire dwelling, they began to throw out old furniture, renovate unoccupied rooms, install new conveniences. And the more daring were ready to abandon the old mansion altogether in order to start life afresh—at least spiritually—in the wilderness or even on the moon.

Writing to his friend Michel de Montaigne, Étienne de la Boétie said: "When at the threshold of our century a new world rose out of the ocean, it happened because the gods wished to create a refuge where men under a better sky can cultivate their fields, while the cruel sword and ignominious plague condemn Europe to perish." A similar mood, a similar desire to make a fresh start, united the scientists with the inventors, starry-eyed writers of utopias with swaggering pioneer backwoodsmen. The New World vision seemed to enlarge and exalt every human possibility, even though the explorers and pioneers, in turning their backs on the Old World, did not in fact leave the "cruel sword" or the "ignominious plague" behind them, for their smallpox, measles, and tuberculosis decimated those natives whom their guns did not exterminate.

When the active period of discovery and colonization was over and the Promised Land still lay below the horizon, much of the original faith and fervor was transferred from the exploitation of the indigenous New World to that of the machine. But, in fact, these two different approaches to the New World—one aimed at natural resources to be discovered and appropriated, the other at mechanical power and artificial wealth to be fabricated and sold profitably—had never been far apart.

At the beginning I suggested that the two forms of exploration, terrestrial and technological, had a common source and long remained in constant interplay. For a few centuries Western man, or at least a wakeful minority, believed it would be possible to make the best of both worlds. We are now sufficiently far away from the original New World pictures, which linger only as afterimages, to see that they did in fact have much in common.

Both movements, to begin with, were characterized by an unconcealed hostility to the past—though to different parts of the past; they openly gloried in discontinuity, if not in outright destruction. In the eighteenth century these contrasting attitudes were summed up in the personalities of Jean Jacques Rousseau and Denis Diderot, the first exalting the primitive, the unsophisticated, and the older peasant folkways, despising formalized order, and favoring spontaneity and simplicity; the second, though personally hankering after the open sexual freedom of the Polynesians, trusting rather to the intelligence than to instincts and natural feelings and eagerly investigating the processes of mechanical invention and production. The fact that these two men began as friends only underlines their symbolic roles.

Beneath both attitudes toward the past was the realization, which had appeared at earlier points in history, notably in the sixth century B.C., that formal civilization had somehow gone wrong, that its most successful institutions had retarded and restricted, rather than furthered, the full development of man, though it had made possible the great collective assemblages of man, the power that transformed the environment and energized the mind—enterprises that no earlier tribal community or village had even dared to conceive of.

It was during the Pyramid Age that

the energies and resources of civilized society were first organized by priest-kings under a commission from heaven into what I have called the "megamachine." Ever since that time it had been evident that the state, the official religion, the bureaucracy, the army, those resurgent institutions of civilization, were indeed capable of effecting great constructive transformations of the environment. But the human price of their success was heavy: the class structure, the lifetime fixation of function, the monopoly of land and economic and educational opportunity, the inequalities of property and privilege, the chronic savagery of slavery and war, the fears and obsessions and paranoid ambitions of the ruling classes, culminated in mass destruction and exterminations. In short, a nightmare. Such constant miscarriages of power and organization offset the genuine claims that could be made for this system and raised serious questions, at least in the minds of the oppressed and the enslaved, about the value of civilization itself. These doubts encouraged the notion that if only the past institutions and structures of civilization were destroyed, men would be happy, virtuous, and free. Rousseau expressed this idea in its most extreme form in his prize essay for the academy at Dijon, in which he castigated the demoralizing effects of the arts and sciences, those features of civilization about which people had the fewest doubts.

The notion that many of the ways of civilization are in fact not beneficent but injurious had been expressed in one way or another in many of the axial religions and philosophies and had taken the form of a yearning for a more elemental mode of life—a return to the village, the bamboo grove, the desert, a search for detachment from the compulsions and regimentations demanded by the megamachine as the price of wealth in peace and victory in war.

Once the traumatic effects of civilization were acknowledged, the elder prophets taught, one might be born again and begin life over on a sound basis, defying sterile tradition, framing new laws, exploring strange environments, throwing off old restraints. These impulses were reaffirmed in that great migration to the wilderness areas that marked the colonization of the New World, for the pioneers perforce left civilization behind them and acted, as Longfellow put it, so that "each tomorrow finds us farther than today."

For a brief period, roughly between 1800 and 1860, or at the latest 1880, it seemed that the principles of Rousseau and Diderot might, at least in a few favored areas, be effectively reconciled: the romantic and the utilitarian personality were learning to live side by side, not merely coexisting, but prospering together. The typical figures of this period did not recoil from science, mechanical invention, or industrial organization; on the contrary, they embraced all these new potentialities within the framework of a larger life that included man's natural and his humanistic inheritance. While Thoreau, for example, responded to the natural environment, exploring every wood, field, and riverbank around Concord, he furthered his family business, pencil making, by utilizing a new process for purifying graphite that he had found in a scientific review. This same ready wholeness of response characterizes and unites the other leading minds of this New World galaxy: Audubon, Olmsted, Emerson, Marsh, Melville, Whitman. They were neither hermits nor primitives; but in their minds at least, they had thrown off the frayed and soiled clothes of all previous civilizations.

This New World utopia, this Promised Land, was soon buried under the ashes and cinders that erupted over the entire Western world in the nineteenth century, thanks to the resurrection and intensification of all the forces that had originally brought "civilization" itself into existence. The rise of the centralized state, the expansion of the bureaucracy and the conscript army, the regimentation of the factory system, the depredations of speculative finance, the spread of imperialism, as in the Mexi-can War, and the continued encroachment of slavery—all these negative movements not only sullied the New World dream but brought back on a larger scale than ever the Old World nightmares that the immigrants to America had risked their lives, and often forfeited their fortunes, to escape.

As a result of this setback the "mechanical" New World displaced the "romantic" New World in men's minds; the latter became a mere escapist dream, not a serious alternative to the existing order. For in the meantime, a new god had appeared, and a new religion had taken possession of the mind, and out of this conjunction arose the new mechanical world-picture, which, with every fresh scientific discovery, every successful new invention, displaced both the natural world and the diverse symbols of human culture with an environment cut solely to the measure of the machine. This ideology gave primacy to the denatured and dehumanized environment in which the new technological complex could flourish without being limited by any human interests and values other than those of technology itself. All too soon, a large portion of the human race would virtually forget that there had ever existed any other kind of environment or any alternative mode of life.

Kepler's Dream

ne reason for the failure to understand the radical weaknesses of both aspects of the New Exploration is that the subjective side has been neglected—indeed not even recognized as existing—chiefly because scientists, in overcoming the subjectivism of earlier systems, resolutely denied the many evidences of science's own subjectivity. Yet, at the very outset, this subjectivism was expressed with classic clarity in Kepler's "Dream," which anticipated by more than three centuries the world in which we are now actually living: its empirical knowledge, its practical devices, its compulsive drives, its mystic aspirations—and most remarkably, its rising disillusion.

Kepler embodied in his own person the three great aspects of the New World transformation: the scientific side, in his classic discovery of the unexpectedly ellipsoid course taken by planets around the sun; the religious side, in his open adoration of the sun and the starry sky as a substantial visible equivalent of the fading Christian heaven; and finally, his untrammeled technical imagination. In a day of sailing ships and short-range, inaccurate cannon he dared to depict in vividly realistic terms the first power-driven journey to the moon. If Kepler was a sun worshiper, he was also as moon-mad as any of the contemporary technicians in the National Aeronautic and Space Administration.

Those who have seen in scientific and technical advance only a cautious, hardheaded series of steps from one solid tuft of observed facts to another, have not reckoned with these hot subjective pressures. The quick leap in Kepler's mind from purely scientific astronomical exploration to this staggering practical exploit surely helps explain the vulgar engulfment in space fantasies today, now that their realization has proved feasible.

The fact that these fantasies should have appeared, fully fleshed, in Kepler's mind at the very moment that the first halting theoretical advances were being made, would seem to indicate that they issued from deep common sources in the collective psyche. The same self-confidence, the same ambitious or aggressive impulse, that sustained a Cortes in the subjugation of Mexico was also working in the leading minds in astronomy and mechanics, if in a more subtle and sublimated form.

Now the remarkable fact about Kepler's moon exploration, apart from the audacity of the conception itself, was his keen grasp of the embarrassing details. He had already canvassed in his mind some of the most serious obstacles to its accomplishment, though he knew quite well that the solution of these problems was beyond the technical knowledge of his age. "On such a headlong dash," he pointed out, "we can take few human companions. . . . The first getting into motion is very hard on him, for he is twisted and turned just as if, shot from a cannon, he were sailing across mountains and seas. Therefore he must be put to sleep beforehand with narcotics and opiates, and he must be arranged, limb by limb, so that the shock will be distributed over the individual members, lest the upper part of his body be carried away from the fundament, or his head be torn from his shoulder. Then comes a new difficulty: terrific cold and difficulty in breathing. . . . Many further difficulties arise, which would be too numerous to recount. Absolutely no harm befalls us."

That this extravagant dream was not so easily translated into the practical world as Kepler impatiently anticipated is far less surprising than the fact that it took possession of Kepler's mind at such an early date. All the forces that had been set in motion by the exploration of our own planet were eventually transferred, with no loss of momentum and no great change of method or goal, to interplanetary exploration—but accompanied likewise by the same defects: the same exorbitant pride, the same aggressiveness, the same disregard for more significant human concerns, and the same insistence upon scientific discovery, technical ingenuity, and rapid locomotion as the chief ends of man. What we also know now, as Kepler could not know, is that space exploration has required a megamachine of far larger dimensions than any previously known one to ensure its success, and that this megamachine has taken centuries to assemble.

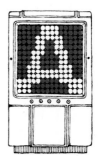

stronomy prepared the groundwork for the great technical transformation that took place after the close of the sixteenth century, for it provided the frame for a depersonalized world-picture within which mechanical activities and interests took precedence over more human concerns. The organization of this world picture was largely the work of a series of mathematicians and physicists who count among the great luminaries of all times. Beginning with Copernicus, Kepler, Galileo, and Descartes, and culminating in Leibnitz and Newton, their systematic descriptions of space, time, motion, mass, and gravitation eventually brought about a major shift in technology: from the workshop to the laboratory, from the tool-using craftsman or artist, himself a prime mover as well as a designer, to the complex power-driven automatic machine under centralized direction and remote control. And it was this world picture, not individual mechanical inventions alone, that contributed to the final apotheosis of the contemporary megamachine.

What was implicit in this new world-picture was something that Galileo would hardly have dared to put into words, even if he had been aware of it. To understand the physical world, and ultimately man himself—who exists in this world as merely a product of mass and motion—one must eliminate the living soul. At the center of the new world-picture man himself did not exist, indeed he had no reason for existence. Instead of man, a creature with a long history on a planet whose inhabitants and habitats have had an immeasurably longer history, only a fragment of man remained—the detached intelligence; and only certain special products of that sterilized intelligence, scientific theorems and machines, could claim any permanent place or any high degree of reality. In the interests of "objectivity" the new scientist eliminated historical man and all his subjective activities. Since Galileo's time this distorted form of subjectivity has been known as "objective science."

By his exclusive preoccupation with quantity Galileo had, in effect, *disqualified* the real world of experience; and he had thus driven man out of living nature into a cosmic desert, even more peremptorily than Jehovah had driven Adam and Eve out of the Garden of Eden. But in Galileo's case the punishment for eating the apple of the tree of knowledge lay in the nature of knowledge itself, for that tasteless, desiccated fruit was incapable of sustaining or reproducing life. One vast tract of the real world, the world of living organisms, was excluded from the province of the exact sciences. The qualities and configurations that belonged most distinctly to that world, along with human history and human culture, were dismissed as "subjective," since only a minute part could be reduced to abstract "sense data" or described in mathematical terms. Only cadavers and skeletons were suitable candidates for scientific treatment. At the same time, the "material" world, that is, the abstract world of "physical objects," operating in an equally abstract space and time, was treated as if it alone had reality.

Though Galileo's interpretation of planetary movements led to a charge of heresy by the Roman Catholic Church, the heresy that he was accused of was one he did not utter. As he plaintively put it at the end of the *Dialogues on Two Worlds,* he could not be justly convicted of a crime he had never committed. Like so many eminent later colleagues in science, such as Pascal, Newton, and Faraday, he was a theological conservative; and even in science he had no notion of bringing about any revolutionary overthrow of previously established truths—his error there, if anything, was to attempt clumsily to shore up and repair Ptolemy's traditional structure.

But actually Galileo committed a crime far graver than any the dignitaries of the Church accused him of; his real crime was that of trading the totality of human experience—not merely the accumulated dogmas and doctrines of the Church—for that small portion that could be observed within a limited time-span and interpreted in terms of such abstract symbols as mass and motion, while denying the unmediated realities of human experience, from which science itself is only a refined ideological derivative. When Galileo divided the realm of human life into two spheres, a subjective sphere, which he chose to exclude from science, and an objective sphere, freed theoretically from man's visible presence but known through rigorous mathematical analysis, he was dismissing as unreal the cultural accretions of meaning that had made mathematics—itself a purely subjective distillation—possible.

For the better part of three centuries scientists followed Galileo's lead. Under the naive belief—exposed by Stallo a century ago—that they were free from metaphysical preconceptions, the orthodox exponents of science suppressed every evidence of human and organic behavior that could not be neatly fitted into their mechanical world-picture. They thus committed, in reverse, the error of the early Christian Fathers who had suppressed any interest in the natural world in order to concentrate upon the fate of the human soul in eternity. That "mass" and "motion" had no more objective existence than "soul" and "immortality," apart from their ascribed relationship to other human experiences, was not even suspected by those who strained at the theological gnat and swallowed the scientific bat. Galileo, in all innocence, had surrendered man's historic birthright: man's memorable, and remembered, experience.

From the seventeenth century on, the technological world, which prided itself on reducing or extruding the human personality, progressively displaced both nature and human culture and claimed indeed a higher status for itself, as the concrete working-model of scientific truth. "In 1893," Loren Eiseley reminds us, "Robert Monro in an opening address before the British Association for the Advancement of Science, remarked sententiously . . . 'imagination, conceptions, idealizations, the moral faculties . . . may be compared to parasites that live at the expense of their neighbors.'" To have pointed the way to this devaluation of the personality, and its eventual exile, was the real crime of Galileo.

The
Pentagon
of
Power

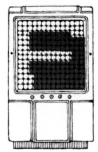

or those who responded to the mechanical world-picture, the extension of the machine to every possible human activity was more than a device to lift the burden of labor or increase wealth. As the otherworldly concerns of religion faded, these new activities were what gave fresh meaning to life, no matter how unfortunate the actual results might seem to be after any cold rational appraisal. Here again one sees, as long before in the Pyramid Age, how the process of mechanization was furthered by an ideology that gave absolute precedence and cosmic authority to the machine itself.

When an ideology conveys such universal meanings and commands such obedience, it has become, in fact, a religion, and its imperatives have the dynamic force of a myth. Those who would question its principles or defy its orders do so at their peril, as groups of rebellious workers continued to discover for the next three or four centuries. From the beginning of the nineteenth century, this refurbished religion united thinkers of the most diverse temperaments, backgrounds, and superficial beliefs: minds as different as Marx and Ricardo, Carlyle and Mill, Comte and Spencer, subscribed to its doctrines; and the working classes, finding themselves helpless to resist these new forces, countered the capitalistic and militaristic expressions of this myth with myths of their own—those of socialism, anarchism, and communism—under which the machine would be exploited not for a ruling elite but for the benefit of the proletarian masses. Against this machine-conditioned utopia only a handful of heretics, mostly poets and artists, dared to hold out.

In English, by a happy alliterative accident, the main components of the new power complex all start with the same initial letter, beginning with the word "Power" itself, so that one may call it—all the more accurately because of contemporary American overtones—the Pentagon of Power. The basic ingredient of this complex has always been power itself, starting in the Pyramid Age with an assemblage of manpower such as no earlier group had been capable of bringing into existence. Over the ages this has been augmented by horsepower, water power, wind power, wood power, coal power, electric power, oil power, and climactically, only yesterday, by nuclear power, itself the ultimate form of the power from chemical reactions that had made the motor and the rocket possible.

Organized political power—backed ultimately by manpower—is the source of both property and productivity: first of all, in the cultivation of the land, using sun power, and then, at later stages, in every other mode of production. Mechanical productivity, linked to increase of power, spells Profit; and without the dynamic stimulus of profit, that is, money power, the system could not so rapidly expand. This perhaps explains why cruder forms of the megamachine, which favored the military caste rather than the merchant and industrial producer and relied on tribute and pillage, remained static, and in the end, unproductive and unprofitable to the point of repeated bankruptcy. Finally, no less an integral part of the power system is Publicity (Prestige, Panache), through which the merely human directors of the power complex —the military, bureaucratic, industrial, and scientific elite—are inflated to more than human dimensions in order to better maintain authority.

These separate components of the power system derive from the far richer ecological complex—"ecosystem," in scientific parlance—in which all organisms, including man, live and move and have their being. Within this ecosystem, which includes human culture, all these components of the power complex originally had their place and performed their indispensable functions. What the power complex did was to wrench the components from their organic matrix and enclose them in an isolated subsystem centered not on the support and intensification of life but on the expansion of power.

So closely are the components of the power complex related that they perform virtually interchangeable functions, in the sense not only that every operation is reducible to pecuniary terms but also that money itself in turn can be translated equally into power or property or publicity or public (television) personalities. This interchangeability of the power components was already plain to Heraclitus at the critical moment that the new money economy was in formation. "All things may be reduced to fire," he observed, "and fire to all things, just as goods may be turned into gold and gold into goods."

When any one of these components is weak or absent, or is not closely enough joined to the neighboring processes, the power system cannot work at full speed or with maximum efficiency. But its final goal is a quantitative abstraction—money, or its etherealized and potentially limitless equivalent, credit. The latter, like the "faith" of the Musical Banks in Erewhon, is at bottom only a pious belief that the system will continue to work indefinitely.

Commitment to the entire power complex, and constant pursuit of pecuniary gains in both direct and indirect forms, define the power system and prescribe its only acceptable goal. That goal, fitly enough, belongs to the same memorable series of alliterations—Progress. In terms of the power system, progress simply means more power, more profit, more productivity, more property, more publicity—all convertible into standard quantitative units. Even publicity can be expressed in column yards of newspaper clippings and man-hours of television appearances. Each new achievement of the power system, whether in scientific research, in education or medicine, in antibiotics, or in space exploration, will be expressed through the same media for institutional magnification and ego-inflation. The school, the church, the factory, the art museum—each currently plays the same power theme, marching to the same beat, saluting the same flags, joining the interminable columns already assembled on the side streets to become the leaders of the great parade that the kings and despots, the conquistadors, the financiers, and the despots of the Renaissance first marshaled together.

Though the constellation that has formed the power system was not deliberately assembled at any single moment, many of its active components, created in earlier civilizations, had, in fact, never passed out of existence. Once the restraining codes and ideals of a more humanly conditioned ideology were destroyed, the power system, freed from such institutions, swiftly burgeoned—in the way that a single biological species taken out of its original habitat and placed in a land with no natural enemies or environmental limitations flourishes at the expense of a multitude of native forms.

The power system has often been mistakenly identified with feudalism, with absolute monarchy, with princely despotism, with capitalism, with fascism, with communism, even with the welfare state. But this multiple identification points to a more important characteristic: the fact that the power complex increasingly underlies *all* these institutional structures; and as it knits more closely together, and seizes more power, and governs wider areas, it tends to suppress original cultural differences that once, under feebler political institutions, were visible.

The
Air-Conditioned
Pyramids

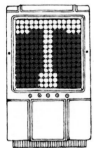

he perfect symbols of the ancient megamachine were the pyramids and the ziggurats. The Egyptian structures were so solidly built, so craftily planned, that they have outlasted all the other architectural works of man; and so well identified are their remains that we can follow the increases in size and engineering skill within the incredibly short period of the three centuries necessary for their complete development.

Though the Pyramid Age had a static conception of heaven, its dynamism was as methodical and relentless as that of our own technocratic age. Each Pharaoh built a new capital for himself within his own lifetime—a practice no present ruler has ventured to imitate. While the pyramids, with their attendant temples and priestly housing facilities, absorbed the surplus energies of the Nile valley, they not only kept this emerging economy of abundance in balance but served as material evidence of the supernatural potencies of the new cosmic religion.

The modernized megamachine has reproduced all the early features of the ancient form by pyramid-building on an even larger scale. And just as the static physical structures supported the worshiper's belief in the validity of the Pharaoh's claims to divinity and immortality, so the new dynamic forms of the pyramid complex—the skyscrapers, the atomic reactors, the nuclear weapons, the superhighways, the space rockets, the underground control centers, the collective nuclear shelters (tombs)—seem equally to validate and exalt the new religion. No other religion has ever produced so many manifestations of power, has brought about such a complete system of control, has unified so many separate institutions, has suppressed so many independent ways of life, or for that matter has ever claimed so many worshipers who by word and deed have testified to the kingdom, the power, and the glory of its nuclear and electronic gods. The miracles performed by the technocratic priesthood are genuine; only their claims of divinity are spurious.

Symbolically, at the entrance to the new pyramid complex stands the nuclear reactor, which first manifested its powers to the multitude by a typical trick of Bronze Age deities: the instant extermination of all the inhabitants of a populous city. Of this early display of nuclear power, as of all the vastly augmented potentialities for destruction that so rapidly followed, one can say what Melville's mad captain in *Moby Dick* says of himself: "All my means and methods are sane: my purpose is mad." For the splitting of the atom was the beautiful consummation —and the confirmation—of the experi-

mental and mathematical modes of thinking that since the seventeenth century have inordinately increased the human command of physical forces.

With the neatness of a Euclidean demonstration, the energy of the sun was now united with the smaller concentrations of energy at man's command; the sun-god had, in effect, undergone a human incarnation, and his priests at last commanded a commensurate authority. Theirs was a Calvinist theology, only slightly revised, in which the mass of men were predestined to awful damnation, and only the elect—the technocratic elite—would be saved. Thus, the eschatology of Jehovah's Witnesses brought up to date.

Once the secret of nuclear fission was unlocked, the construction of the new pyramids went on at such a furious rate that within a dozen years the United States military strategists were forced to invent a new term, "overkill," to describe the superfluous powers of extermination they already possessed. On a planet holding perhaps three billion people, they had bombs enough to wipe out three hundred billion. In this new abundance, the means of death outpaced the means of life.

Even at the risk of seeming to push the parallel between the ancient Pyramid Age and the modern one too far, I would suggest that the manned space capsule, as now conceived, corresponds exactly to the innermost chamber of the great pyramids, where the mummified body of the Pharaoh, surrounded by the miniaturized equipment necessary for travel to heaven, was placed.

Already, in preparation for explorations outside the solar system, some of the priests of science have conjured up anew the assurance of an artificially contrived immortality, necessary for traveling distances that must be measured in light-years. They assume that at such astral speeds living organisms would become comatose and shrink in mass, according to Einstein's theorem, without suffering any internal damage or experiencing the passage of time: so that a thousand years would pass as a day, and vital processes would be similarly reduced and suspended. Again this parallel between the motivations and symbolisms of the two ages is almost too precise to seem anything but a perverse invention. But fortunately the data is open to public investigation.

What space technics has already achieved within the insulated capsule may be described as temporary mummification: a state that provides the minimal conditions for keeping the human agent alive, or rather, from decomposing in the course of his flight. If the Egyptian tomb may be properly described as a static rocket, the cosmic space rocket is in fact a mobile tomb. In each case the most exquisite confections of technology have been provided to keep a human mannequin in a state of suspended animation.

At the bottom of this whole effort lies a purpose that animates the entire megamachine, and indeed, figures as its only viable consummation: to reduce the human organism itself, its habitat, its mode of existence, and its life purpose to just those minimal dimensions that will bring it under total external control. The isolation cells in nineteenth-century prisons were the first approach to this ideal state—but were used only as extreme punishment.

In the case of the Egyptian Pharaoh, those who placed him in his heaven-pointed spaceship made believe that he was still alive and capable of exercising all his exalted faculties. But just the opposite set of assumptions governs the preparations of an astronaut for a space voyage: while actually alive, he is forced under strict training to divest himself of every hampering attribute of life, so that what is left of human existence are just those minimal bodily and mental functions that will enable him to survive under hardships and deprivations as formidable as those encountered by the climbers who topped Mount Everest in the final ascent.

Obviously, only a mixture of adventurous impulses and religious convictions of the deepest sort would persuade "normal," warmhearted human beings, such as many astronauts seem to be, to take part in such a life-denying ritual. Besides high physical courage, and the promise of an early termination of the ordeal, they need a deep religious conviction, all the more serviceable if unconscious, of their role as Heavenly Messengers. A devotion of this order made it possible for a Christian hermit to wall himself permanently within a dark, fetid hut, to be fed only through a vent; so the mode of sacrifice is not without earlier holy precedent. But nothing more eloquently testifies to the hold the myth of the machine has established than the acceptance of this ritual as a desirable and laudable "next step" in man's denatured command of nature.

Up to the present it is the negative results of the great scientific achievement of splitting the atom that are colossal. As far as the nuclear bombs themselves go, the only positive benefits are those that temporarily accrue to the industrial, bureaucratic, and scientific establishments that have built up the new megamachine. Paradoxically, then, the greatest gains that have been achieved through command of nuclear reactions have been purely spiritual ones: an enriched conception of cosmic realities, a deeper insight into the nature of the universe and of the place that living organisms, and man himself, have come to occupy.

In the end the most disastrous consequence of the building of the nuclear pyramid may turn out to be neither nuclear weapons themselves nor some irretrievable act of extermination that they may bring about. Something even worse may be in store, and should it go far enough, be equally irretrievable —namely, the universal imposition of the megamachine, in a perfected form, as the ultimate instrument of pure "intelligence," whereby every other manifestation of human potentiality will be suppressed or completely eliminated. Already the blueprints for that structure are available; they have even been advertised as man's highest destiny.

Yet, happily for mankind, the mega-machine itself is in trouble, largely because of its early dependence upon the nuclear bomb. For the very concept of wielding absolute power has set a collective trap so delicately balanced that its mechanism has more than once been on the point of snapping down on its appointed victims, the inhabitants of the planet. Had that happened, the megamachine would have shattered its own structure as well. Over the entire Pentagon of Power, thanks to the technocratic arrogance and automated stupidity of those who have built this citadel, hovers a nuclear Ragnarok, or Twilight of the Gods, long ago predicted in Norse mythology: a world consumed in flames, when all things human and divine will be overcome by the cunning dwarfs and the brutal giants. After the Sixth Dynasty the Pyramid Age in Egypt ended in a violent popular uprising, even without any such cosmic disruption. And something less than the Norse nightmare, though no less ominous to the megamachine, may be in store—*or is it now perhaps actually taking place?*

The
New
Organum
of
Life

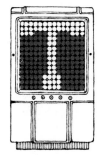

he great revolution needed to save mankind from the projected assaults against life by the controllers of the megamachine demands first of all a displacement of the mechanical world-picture and its replacement by an organic world-picture, in the center of which stands man himself—"cool and composed" as Walt Whitman says, "before a million universes."

If we are to prevent megatechnics from further controlling and deforming every aspect of human culture, we shall be able to do so only with the aid of a radically different model derived directly, not from machines, but from living organisms and organic and social complexes (ecosystems). What can be known about life only through the process of living—and so is part of the experience of even the humblest of organisms—must be added to all the other aspects that can be observed and abstracted.

This new model will in time replace megatechnics with biotechnics, the first step toward passing from power to plenitude. Once an organic world-picture is in the ascendant, the working aim of an economy of plenitude would be not to feed more human functions into the machine but to further develop man's incalculable potentialities for self-actualization and self-transcendence, taking back into himself deliberately many of the activities he has too. supinely surrendered to the system.

Under the power complex the purely quantitative concept of unlimited abundance, not merely material but also symbolic abundance, has served as the guiding principle. In opposition to this, an organic system directs itself to qualitative richness, amplitude, spaciousness, freedom from quantitative pressure and crowding, since self-regulation, self-correction, and self-propulsion are as much an integral property of organisms as nutrition, reproduction, growth, and repair. Balance, wholeness, completeness, continuous interplay between the inner and the outer, the subjective and the objective, aspects of existence, are identifying characteristics of the organic model, and the general name for an economy based on such a model is an economy of plenitude—plenitude as distinct from mere excess, affluence, or abundance.

The chief properties of a power system—the magnification and overextension of power alone and the lack of qualifications and boundaries—are antithetic to those of an organic system. In organisms power is always related to function and purpose. Life does not flourish under a regime of compulsive dynamism, where uncontrolled change —change only for the sake of further change, such as megatechnics now imposes—removes the possibility of either maintaining a dynamic equilibrium or else going on with any autonomous development.

The notion that the megamachine is in fact omnipotent and irresistible came in, as we have seen, with the cult of divine kingship: the ancient myth of the machine. At the entrances to the great palaces in Mesopotamia and Egypt from which the ancient system was governed, there were stationed gigantic statues of lions or bulls, whose main object was to fill those who approached the royal presence with a paralyzing sense of their own littleness and impotence, as a tomb text of the fourteenth to twelfth century B.C. said of the intentions of the sun-god Re: *"I shall prevail over them as a King and diminish them."* In more devious symbolic ways these same awe-inspiring creatures still stand at the portals of the Pentagon of Power today, though the god they represent, whose secret knowledge cannot be challenged and whose divine commands cannot be questioned, turns out actually to be, when one tears aside the curtain, only the latest model IBM computer, zealously programmed by Dr. Strangelove and his assistants.

But there is another error, the reverse of magnifying the role of power, that it would be equally fatal to make, and one that now tempts the younger generation: the notion that in order to avoid the predictable calamities that the power complex is bringing about, one must destroy the whole fabric of historical civilization and begin all over again on an entirely fresh foundation. Unfortunately, that "fresh founda-tion," as envisaged by such revolutionary groups, includes the forms of mass communication, mass transportation, and mass indoctrination that favor, not human liberation, but a mass dictatorship, one that is possibly even more dehumanized than the present affluent Establishment, since it renounces as both worthless and irrelevant our immense cultural accumulations. As if ignorance and impotence were viable solutions!

What applies to ancient Bronze Age civilizations, and partly atones for their misuse of power, applies equally to our modern equivalents. "The negative institutions... would never have endured so long but for the fact that their positive goods, even though they were arrogated to the use of the dominant minority, were ultimately of service to the whole community, and *tended to produce a universal society of far higher potentialities, by reason of its size and diversity.*" If that observation held true at the beginning, it is even more true today, now that this remarkable technology has spread over the whole planet. The only way to effectively overcome the power system is to transfer its more helpful agents to an organic complex. And it is in and through the human person that the invitation to plenitude begins and ends.

For its effective salvation mankind will need something like a religious conversion, one that will replace the mechanical world-picture with an organic world-picture and give to the human personality as the highest known manifestation of life, the precedence it now gives to machines and computers. This order of change is as hard for most people to conceive of as was the change from the classic power-complex to that of Christianity, or later, from supernatural medieval Christianity to the machine-modeled ideology of the seventeenth century. But such changes have repeatedly occurred all through history, and under catastrophic pressure they may occur again. Of only one thing can we be confident: if mankind is to escape self-extinction, the God who saves us will not descend from the machine; he will rise up again in the human soul.

The Human Way Out

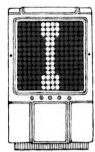

I f we are to save technology itself from the aberrations of its present leaders and putative gods, we must, in both our thinking and our acting, come back to the human center, for it is here, and only here, that all significant transformations begin and terminate. What Goethe said about nature applies equally to every manifestation of culture and personality: "Nature has neither core nor skin: she's both at once outside and in." It is on that assumption that I have given equal weight, in describing man's technological advances, to every part of his organism, not to the hand and its derivative tools alone. And this is why, too, I have emphasized the part played by wishes and projects, by symbols and fantasies, upon even the most practical applications of technology. For it is through all the activities of the mind, not the intelligence and the dynamic instruments of intelligence alone, that radical departures from conventional practices are made in technics itself.

This approach, if sound, carries with it a conclusion that challenges those who imagine that the forces and institutions now in existence will go on indefinitely, becoming bigger and more powerful, even though their very bigness and power threaten to nullify the benefits originally sought. If human culture in fact arises, develops, and renews

itself through fresh activities in the mind, it may be modified and transformed by the same processes. What the human mind has created, it can also destroy. Neglect or withdrawal of interest works as effectively as physical assault. This is a lesson that our machine-oriented world must quickly assimilate if it is to preserve even its own successful innovations.

In order to describe the active part man has played in his technical development—as contrasted with the view that he is the fated victim of external forces and external institutions over which he has little or no control—I purpose to follow the interplay of man's subjective and objective life in two complementary movements: materialization and etherealization. Paradoxically, the process of materialization begins in the mind, while that of etherealization proceeds from the visible and external world to the inner personality, finally taking form in the mind, through words and other symbols, as a more or less coherent world-view.

The first phase of materialization springs from neural activities to which the term "mind" can hardly yet be attached; what later will come forth as an "idea" might with greater accuracy be called an apparition, more impalpable than the traditional ghost. This apparition is, by definition, an entirely private experience, unformed, wordless, incommunicable—and therefore more difficult to lay hold of than even a nocturnal dream. Obviously such an intuitive process cannot be investigated scientifically; its existence can only be deduced by a backward reading from its later developments. But the constant flow of stimuli from the internal organs of the body, including the brain itself, which shows activity even in sleep, must be posited as the starting point for all formalized and organized mental life.

The existence of these formless subjective activities might remain questionable were it not for the fact that they have a tendency, if heeded—and especially if frequently repeated—to

take on a stable character. Thus, the nascent "idea" of courage, before it can be called an idea, may assume the recallable image of a lion. To pass from what is internal, unconscious, and private, to a public world that can be shared by other men is the next stage in materialization. At this point the nascent idea, well before it can find words to do so, expresses itself in the language of the body. It is by this process that formative ideas that may eventually dominate a whole society take possession of a living person and in time become visible to other men.

Most germinal ideas die a-borning; they never pass beyond the stage of apparition. Even an idea viable enough and lucky enough to survive must undergo a long period of incubation and experimental testing before it becomes sufficiently palpable as an idea to get lodged, like a wind-blown seed, in a niche favorable to its growth. That niche must be a living person, though not always the originator and only begetter. This is the phase of "incarnation."

Even before an idea can be transmitted in speech it becomes, if one may use the classic New Testament description, incarnate in the flesh, and makes itself known by appropriate bodily changes. Do not suppose that the preliminary phases of intuition and ideation are in any sense mystical: they are commonplaces of everyday experience. Nor does the concept of incarnation refer necessarily to the particular theological epiphany from which we derive the term. In ancient times the idea of kingship arose as a transcendental image of power and authority derived from a fusion of the commanding experience of a mighty hunting chief with the worship of a solar deity, Atum-Re—or in Sumer and Akkad, with an equally powerful storm-god who there took precedence.

But we need not look to ancient Mesopotamia, Egypt, or Palestine for examples of incarnation. The yearning for a primitive counter-culture, defying the rigidly organized and deper-

15

sonalized forms of Western civilization, began to float into the Western mind in the original expressions of romanticism among the intellectual classes. That desire to return to a more primeval state took a folksy, if less articulate, form in the elemental rhythms of jazz more than half a century ago. What made this idea suddenly erupt again into Western society, with almost volcanic power, was its incarnation in the Beatles. It was not just the sudden success of the Beatles' recordings that indicated a profound change was taking place in the minds of the young; it was their new personality, expressed in their long, neo-medieval haircut, their unabashed sentimentality, their nonchalant posture, and their dreamlike spontaneity, that opened up for the postnuclear generation the possibility of an immediate escape from megatechnic society. In the Beatles, all their repressions, and all their resentments of repression, were released. By hairdo, costume, ritual, and song, all changes depending upon purely personal choice, the new ideas that bound the younger generation together were at once clarified and magnified. Ideas that were still too dumbly felt to be expressed in words spread like wildfire through incarnation and imitation.

The spread of a new gospel through visible personalities often characterizes the emergence of a new cultural epoch. There were many Messiahs and teachers of righteousness, genuine and false, both before and after the coming of Jesus Christ.

But note: the newly incarnated personality, be it Buddhist or Liverpool-Dionysian, cannot survive alone, narcissistically gazing at its own image. Like a single biological mutant, the idea would be doomed unless similar impulses were beginning to find corporeal form in thousands of other personalities. Through this general readiness, in fact, the formative idea must imprint itself, by direct contact and emulation, upon a sufficient body of disciples and followers before the idea

itself in more purely verbal form can be understood. Whitman spoke for all participators in this process when he said, "I and mine do not convince by arguments: we convince by our presence." Proverbially, it is first by living the life that one knows the doctrine: by taking visible bodily shape the idea begins to spread throughout the community by word of mouth, long before it can be more effectively defined in written statements and philosophical formulations.

The next stage, toward a wider socialization of the idea, may be called "incorporation." At this point the original formative impulse is reinforced by conscious rational effort throughout the whole community, manifesting itself in the habits of the family, the customs of the village, the routines of the city, the practices of the workshop, the rituals of the temple, the legal procedures of the court. Without this general social adoption and modification, the formative idea, even if widely incarnated, would lose its authority and efficacy. Indeed, it was the failure of Christianity to extend its moral principles to organized government, its reluctance to come to grips with slavery and war and class exploitation, despite the immense energies it released in other departments, that was responsible for its loss of impetus, its inner corrosion, and its failure to achieve the universal brotherly society that it had proclaimed.

Karl Marx properly recognized how effective a role the organization of the materials of production (technology) played in molding the human personality. But he made the grave error of treating economic organization as an independent, self-evolving factor, immune to active human intervention; whereas this form of materialization is but one of the many ways in which the fermenting ideas of a culture become accepted, regularized, and carried into general daily practice. In this respect, perhaps, the high point of Christian social achievement came relatively late

in the Middle Ages, when its monasteries, convents, almshouses, orphanages, and hospitals were to be found in every city and town, on a scale hitherto unknown.

It is by institutional extension that subjective impulses cease to be private, willful, contradictory, and ineffectual and become capable of bringing about large social changes. Matriarchy in one age, kingship in another, divine redemption and salvation in a third, must be incorporated into every institution and influence every collective action if the formative ideas underlying an emerging culture are to flourish sufficiently and hold their own against the mass of residues and encrusted material survivals, still tenacious and often powerful. It is only by this act of incorporation that the assent and support of a larger population can be assured.

At this point of incorporation the new cultural form, for better and worse, loses some of its original purity. Those who have fallen under the spell of a new vision, or who have sought to take on swiftly the mask of a new personality, often shrink from accepting this further mode of materialization—it seems at best a compromise, at worst a complete betrayal. Certainly by incorporation into existing institutions, the idea does lose some of its original purity, if it does not in fact turn into its own antithesis through the very act of materialization.

Thus, when the Roman state was converted to Christianity under Constantine, the Christian church was also converted in some degree to paganism, and not merely tolerated many Roman practices but even transferred the sadistic rituals of the Roman arena to the Christian conception of hell as an ultimate dispensation of divine justice, making the spectacle of the eternal torture of condemned sinners one of the supreme joys for the faithful souls in heaven.

The final materialization of a formative idea, from its preconscious inception in many individual minds to a fully externalized and socialized state shared by everyone, consists in the transformation of the physical environment, through practical means and symbolic expressions alike. This phase may be called "embodiment." First, the plot is outlined and the actors chosen; then the actors put on their make-up and their costumes; next, the scenario is outlined and the plot developed; and finally, new physical structures are built in order to express and support the idea.

Yet it is in these reconstituted physical structures that novel possibilities are revealed that were only latent in the original conception—quite untranslatable into more easily formed verbal, graphic, or musical symbols. Could Jesus Christ, the most spontaneous and informal of personalities, have guessed that the ultimate expression of Christianity would be realized in a formalized hierarchic organization, operating uniformly over the entire continent of Europe, and that the culmination of this worldly movement would be the widespread erection of cathedrals, churches, and monasteries whose technical audacity and aesthetic vitality had no place in Jesus' intuitions? And yet, paradoxically, without the Christian idea there would have been no Durham, no Chartres, no Bamberg—and no Inquisition! What better revelation could be offered of the unpredictability of the future—as contrasted with the present method of extrapolating observable existing tendencies.

Though I have used a particular episode in Western history, the rise of the Christian church, as a convenient example, the process summarized is a general one, applicable with many variations to all cultures, not least to the triumph of the myth of the machine.

In putting together the phases of materialization in a serial form in time, I have ignored simultaneous phenomena and have treated as if they were separate and formally recognizable, events, institutions, personalities, and ideas that were in fact in constant flux and interaction, undergoing both inner and outer transformations. So, for example, the incarnation of Jesus did not take place only once; the Christian idea, to be kept alive, needed further reincarnations, always with fresh modifications, in the persons of Paul, Augustine, Francis of Assisi, and countless other Christian souls.

In these changes, the luminous original message lost, no doubt, some of its force, for the ideas suitable to a dying culture were irrelevant to the resurgent vitalities of later periods. Yet, though both the institutional organization of the Church and its wealth of physical structures smothered the original flame, it smoldered on—and astonishingly flared up again in our own late day in the person of Pope John XXIII.

One final aspect of materialization remains to be noted: a paradox. And this is that subjective expressions remain alive in the mind far longer than do the corporate organizations and physical buildings that seem to the outward eye to be so solid and durable. Even when a culture disintegrates, the loss is never quite complete or final. From the total achievement much will remain and leave its imprint on later minds, in the form of sport, play, language, art, customs. Though few Westerners have seen a Hindu temple, the Sanskrit roots for mother and for father still remain on their tongue in addressing their parents, more durable than any monument. This symbolic debris of past cultures forms a rich compost for the mind without which the cultural environment would be as sterile as that of the moon. André Varagnac has demonstrated that an extremely ancient, orally transmitted culture, largely neolithic, perhaps even preneolithic, in origin, passed on its magical beliefs, its sexual customs and marriage rites, its folklore and fairy tales, to succeeding generations throughout the world.

This archaic culture still forms the buried underlayer of contemporary society. The games of ball played today are survivals from the temples, where in religious ritual the ball represented the sun, and the opposing players stood for the forces of light and darkness. The notorious recrudescence of astrology and witchcraft today is only the latest example of this subjective persistence. Even when all the material properties needed for a worn-out drama have disappeared, some vestige of the play itself will remain, in proverbs, ballads, musical phrases, and melodies reverberating from generation to generation—more enduring in the spoken word than if incised in stone.

When the organizing idea of a culture has been fully explored, when its drama has been played out and all that is left of the original creative impulse is a soul-deadening ritual and a compulsory drill, the moment for a new formative idea has come. Against such a change, however, the whole body of entrenched institutions presents a solid wall; for what is an institution but a closed society for the prevention of change? Hence the path of etherealization, so far from beginning with a new idea, starts at just the opposite end by attacking the visible structures and organizations, which, as long as they remain in good working order, allow no place for a new idea to take hold.

The path of etherealization, then, is often opened up by a breakdown that invites this assault. At first this is mainly a physical breakdown, which exposes the technical ineptitude or human insufficiency of a seemingly prosperous society. Wars and the physical impoverishment and destruction that wars produce, along with the depletion of life, epidemic diseases and environmental degradations, soil erosion, pollution, failure of crops, outbreaks of criminal violence and psychotic malevolence—all these are symptoms of such disorganization. And they in turn produce social lapses, for the people affected, feeling cheated and oppressed, refuse to perform their old duties or make the necessary sacrifices always needed for keeping the mechanism of society moving.

What brings on these breakdowns usually turns out to be a radical failure in feedback: an inability to acknowledge errors, an unwillingness to correct them, a resistance to introducing new ideas and methods that would provide the means for a sufficiently radical transformation. If recognized promptly, and if immediate action were taken with the means at hand, many of the defects that eventually undermine a society could be corrected. Failing this, a direr pathological situation, demanding surgery rather than diet, comes into existence.

For these reasons, the first manifestation of etherealization, though it issues from subjective disillusion and disenchantment, does not take place on the level of ideas; it begins rather with an assault upon visible buildings, in acts of iconoclasm and destruction. Sometimes this takes the form of an organized physical attack; sometimes it shows itself by a rejection of the old structures, as when the Christians deserted the Roman arenas and public baths and established themselves in other buildings on other sites. Obviously the visible forms of a society are easier to identify—and to demolish—than the underlying ideas and doctrines, which can be maintained in the mind, as the Jews secretly kept to their ancient rites even in Catholic Spain. But the burning of books and the tearing down of sound buildings undermine confidence in continuity.

Though materialization is necessarily a slow process, dematerialization works fast. Even the cessation of work on new structures, or the rebuilding of them in a new style, as in the daring Gothic constructions that displaced the ponderous Romanesque forms, constitutes an action that, according to the proverb, speaks louder than words.

When the dismantlement has gone far enough, the way will be open for the positive forces of etherealization—for the ground has been sufficiently cleared. At this point, the furnishings and draperies of the existing society will begin, for all their shiny newness,

to seem old-fashioned; and the apartments that were once reserved for the elite will be advertised for occupancy by new tenants—who ironically will either build different quarters for themselves elsewhere or will take possession of even more ancient structures and convert them to their new purposes, in the way that the mansions of the aristocracy in London, Paris, and Rome have been converted into business offices, hotels, and retail establishments for members of the higher bureaucracy.

There is no need to provide further specific historic examples of etherealization. Again, as in the behavior of organisms, the integrating and disintegrating processes take place side by side, not without affecting each other. To follow the course of etherealization, one has only to read the serial analysis of materialization backward—beginning with debuilding and dismantling, and coming back finally to the initial stage, where a change in character and life-style becomes visible—until the point is reached where a formative idea again emerges. For when the negative phase of etherealization has gone far enough, a new constellation of ideas, a new world-picture, a new vision of human possibilities, will take possession of a whole culture, and a different cast of characters will occupy the center of the stage and present a new drama.

If, on the other hand, the processes of disillusion, alienation, dismantlement, and destruction go further, if no counterbalancing modes of etherealization become effective, disintegration will, it seems probable, go on with increasing swiftness until no restorative measures are possible. In this case, the forces of anti-life will be in the ascendant, and the actors who seize the center of the stage and profess to represent the Living Theatre will be incarnations of the absurd, the sadistic, the cruel, and the paranoid, whose mission will be to give the final sanction of their own insanity to the dehumanization that has been achieved by the power complex.

Toward
an
Organic
Society

ortunately, there are already indications, though scattered, faint, and often contradictory, that a fresh transformation is in the making—one that will show the money economy is bankrupt and the power complex has become, through its very excesses and exaggerations, impotent. Whether further disintegration can be arrested, still more whether the nuclear megamachine can be successfully dismantled before it brings on a total human catastrophe, are matters that may long remain in doubt. But if mankind overcomes the myth of the machine, one thing can be safely predicted: the repressed components of our old culture will become the dominants of the new one, and similarly, the present megatechnic institutions and structures will be reduced to human proportions and brought under direct human control. Should this prove true, the present canvass of the existing society, its technological miscarriages and its human misdemeanors, should by implication give valid positive directions for working out a life economy.

If this seems an all but impossible demand, with the odds heavily in favor of the power system and against the human personality, one need only remember how absurd such a withdrawal, such a rejection, such a challenge, seemed to most intelligent Romans before Christianity presented an alternative.

In the period of the first Roman emperor, Augustus (63 B.C.–A.D. 14), the Roman power system, supported and extended by its massive engineering and military machines, reached the height of its authority and influence. Who then guessed that the law and order of the Pax Romana were not so solidly established as to be virtually impregnable? Despite the earlier warnings of the historian Polybius, the Henry Adams of his day, the Romans expected that their way of life would last indefinitely. So well entrenched was their economy that educated Romans long regarded with contempt the insignificant Christian minority who deliberately withdrew from this system, who rejected their goods and disparaged their massive achievements no less than their insensate dedication to gluttony and pornography.

What educated Roman could guess, at the time of Marcus Aurelius, that only two centuries later one of their best-educated minds, Augustine, a lecturer of note, thoroughly at home in the culture of the past, would write *The City of God* to expose the iniquities of the whole Roman establishment and castigate even its virtues? And who then, in his wildest fancies, could guess that a while later Paulinus of Nola, a patrician, born to be a Roman consul, the highest political office open, would retire to a distant Spanish monastery at the height of his career, to cultivate his faith in the divine order and eternal life promised by Jesus, and so believing, would eventually sell himself into slavery in order to ransom from captivity the only son of a widowed mother? Yet that unthinkable ideological transformation did take place, and those unthinkable deeds actually were done.

If such renunciation and detachment could begin in the proud Roman Empire, they can take place anywhere, even here and now—all the more easily today after more than half a century of economic depressions, world wars, revolutions, and systematic programs of extermination have ground the moral foundations of modern civilization to rubble and dust. If the power system itself seems never to have been so formidable as now, with one brilliant technological feat following another,

its negative counterpart of antimatter has never been so threatening. Unqualified violence and crime in every form, patterned after the dehumanized examples of the Pentagon of Power, have invaded what were once the most secure and inviolable human activities. This is not a prophecy; it is a factual description of what is happening before our eyes, with murderous confrontations and infantile tantrums taking the place of rational demands and cooperative efforts. Yes, the physical structure of the power system has never been more closely articulated; but its human supports have never been more frail, indecisive, or vulnerable.

How long, those who are now awake must ask themselves, how long can the physical structure of an advanced technology hold together when its human foundations are crumbling away? This has happened so suddenly that many people are hardly aware that it has happened at all. Yet during the past generation the very bottom has dropped out of our lives; the human institutions and moral convictions that have taken thousands of years to achieve even a minimal efficacy have disappeared.

Let us take a commonplace example of this collapse. What would the great proconsuls of the British Empire, the Curzons, the Cromers, the Milners, have said if, in 1914, they had been informed that despite all the favorable statistical reports in the yearbooks, their Empire would, within a single generation, fall to pieces—though at that very moment Sir Edward Luytens was designing the imposing buildings of the new capital at Delhi and a great viceregal mansion, as if the Empire would hold together for countless centuries? Only Kipling, the poet of imperialism, foresaw this.

How could these empire builders have known what is now so plain, that the most lasting result of British imperialism, in its most humane expression as the Commonwealth of Nations, would be to open the way for a counter-colonialism and a counterinvasion of England by its once subject peoples?

Yet all this has happened, with parallel reversals and humiliations already visible everywhere else, not least in the United States. If these outer bastions of the Pentagon of Power have been taken, how long will it be before the center itself surrenders or blows up?

The Roman Empire in the East won a new lease on life for a thousand years by coming to terms with Christianity. If the power system is to continue in existence as a working partner in a more organic complex dedicated to the renewal of life, it will only be because its dynamic leaders and those larger groups that they influence undergo a profound change of heart and mind, of ideal and purpose, as great as the one that for so long arrested the decay of the Eastern Empire established in Byzantium. But it must be remembered that this intermixture of Roman and Christian institutions was achieved at the expense of creativity. So until the disintegration of our own society has gone even further, there is reason to look for a more vigorous life-promoting solution. Whether such a response is possible depends upon unknown factors: how viable are the formative ideas that are now in the air, and how ready are our contemporaries to undertake the efforts and sacrifices that are essential for human renewal?

Each one of us, as long as life stirs within him, may play a part in extricating himself from the power system by asserting his primacy as a person in quiet acts of mental or physical withdrawal—in gestures of nonconformity, in abstentions, restrictions, inhibitions, that will liberate him from the domination of the Pentagon of Power. In a hundred different places the marks of such dematerialization and etherealization are already visible—many more than I have felt it necessary to cite. If I dare to foresee a more promising future than the one that the technocrats (the power elite) have been confidently extrapolating, it is because I have found by personal experience that it is far easier to detach oneself from the system and to make a selective use of its facilities than the promoters of the Affluent Society would have their docile subjects believe.

Within the past decade many heroic acts of detachment have taken place in the United States, notably among young men who have been called to military service and have courted imprisonment or loss of citizenship by refusing to take part in the Vietnam war, or, when in active service, to carry out the atrocious practices of biocide and genocide dictated by the military command. But other significant acts of detachment and defiance, less heroic but no less threatening to the power system, have taken place at the highest levels of the power hierarchy. Witness the decision of Dr. Norbert Wiener at the end of the Second World War not to put his scientific talents any longer at the disposal of the military machine. At the time, the moral justification for such an act would have been denied by perhaps a majority of Wiener's fellow scientists; but since then, the disaffection has extended from a minority of socially responsible scientists to many of the educational institutions that have allowed themselves to become dependent upon both the governmental and corporate megamachines for vocational opportunities and financial support for research. Though no immediate and sudden escape from the power system is possible, least of all through mass violence, the changes that will restore autonomy and initiative to the human person all lie within the province of the individual soul, once it is roused. Nothing could be more damaging to the myth of the machine, and to the dehumanized social order it has brought into existence, than a steady withdrawal of interest, a slowing down of tempo, a stoppage of senseless routines and mindless acts. And has not all this in fact begun to happen?

Behind the picture of fresh human possibilities I have been drawing stands a truth to which William James gave expression almost a century ago. "When from our present advanced standpoint," he observed, "we look back upon past stages of human thought, we are amazed that a universe which appears to us of so vast and mysterious a complication should ever have seemed to anyone so little and plain a thing. . . . There is nothing in the spirit and principles of science that need hinder science from dealing successfully with a world in which personal forces are the starting point of new effects. The only form of thing we directly encounter, the only experience that we concretely have, is our own personal life. The only complete category of our thinking, our professors of philosophy tell us, is the abstract elements of that. And this systematic denial on science's part of the personality as a condition of events, this rigorous belief that in its own essential and innermost nature our world is a strictly impersonal world, may conceivably, as the whirligig of time goes round, prove to be the very defect that our descendents will be most surprised at in our boasted science, the omission that to their eyes will most tend to make it look perspectiveless and short."

When the moment comes to replace power with plenitude, external mechanical rituals with internal, self-imposed discipline, depersonalization with individuation, automation with autonomy, we shall find that the necessary changes in attitude and purpose have been going on beneath the surface during the past century, and that the long-buried seeds of a richer human culture are now ready to strike root and grow, as soon as the ice breaks up and the sun reaches them. If that growth is to prosper, it will do so by drawing freely on the compost from many previous cultures; and as the power complex itself becomes sufficiently materialized, its formative ideas will become usable again, passing on its intellectual vitality and discipline, once applied mainly to the management of things, to the management and enrichment of man's subjective existence.

As long as man's life prospers there is no limit to its possibilities, no terminus to its creativity, for it is part of the

In our artist's vision (opposite), future Man sits naked and bereft among the ruins of the Pentagon of Power, wondering, perhaps, why he did not heed Lewis Mumford's counsel.

essential nature of man to transcend the limits of his own biological nature and to be ready to die if necessary in order to make such transcendence possible.

The whirligig of time has gone round, and what James applied to science applies equally to our compulsive, depersonalized, power-driven technology. We now have sufficient historical perspective to realize that this seemingly self-automated mechanism has, like the old "automatic" chess-player, a man concealed in the works; and we know that the system is not directly derived from nature as we find it on earth or in the sky, but has limitations that at every point bear the stamp of the human mind, partly rational, partly cretinous, partly demonic. No outward tinkering will improve this overpowered civilization, now plainly in the final and fossilized stage of its materialization; nothing will produce an effective change but the fresh transformation that has already begun in the human mind.

Those who are unable to accept William James's perception that the human person has always been the "starting point for new effects" and that the most solid-seeming structures and institutions must collapse as soon as the formative ideas that have brought them into existence collapse and dissolve, are the real prophets of doom. Within the terms imposed by technocratic society, there is no choice for mankind except to go along with plans for accelerated technological progress, even though man's vital organs will all be cannibalized in order to prolong the megamachine's meaningless existence. But for those of us who have thrown off the myth of the machine, the next move is up to us. The gates of the technocratic prison will open automatically, despite their rusty, ancient hinges, as soon as man chooses to walk out.

DRAWINGS BY CHAS B SLACKMAN

In this painting from the Black Horse Tomb (340–320 B.C.) the horseman's stately ride suggests his journey into the afterlife.

Our First Look At Greek Wall-Painting

A few fragments were all that remained from the great flowering of Hellenic painting in the fourth and fifth centuries B.C., until, in a necropolis outside Paestum, a subterranean art gallery came to light

Suppose all we knew about Shakespeare was that his Elizabethan contemporaries had considered him their greatest playwright. Then suppose that, against all odds, a copy of one of his plays turned up. The excitement such an event would create can be imagined.

Similar excitement has been generated in the past few years by the discovery, outside Paestum in southern Italy, of frescoes painted by Greek artists at a time when Greek civilization was at its height—the first such paintings ever seen by modern man.

The world has always, of course, possessed evidence of the artistic genius of ancient Greece. In architecture, one thinks of the Parthenon in Athens—or the temples of Paestum. Greek sculpture is exhibited in museums everywhere. So is Greek pottery. But until very recently almost no examples had been found of Greek wall-painting—which the Greeks of old considered the noblest expression of their culture.

What had happened to their paintings? It was assumed that they had all been destroyed in antiquity or obliterated by fire, time, or weather. And since the ancient Greeks did not bury their dead in tombs, archaeologists had concluded that their chances of finding

The Temple of Neptune (Poseidon) in Paestum is the best preserved of the three splendid Doric temples that are still standing there.

any Greek wall-paintings were virtually nil.

To understand how this conclusion was upset, it is helpful to know something about when and where the newly found paintings were executed, and by whom.

In about 720 B.C. Greek mariners founded a settlement called Sybaris on the Gulf of Taranto. Sybaris became the first of several cities in a prosperous Greek colony, extending over eastern Sicily and southern Italy, known as Magna Graecia. Its citizens' love of luxury was such that to this day the word "sybarite" means a person devoted to luxury and pleasure.

Like other cities of Magna Graecia,

Sybaris traded with the Etruscans to the north. In about 650 B.C. a group of Sybarites founded a city called Poseidonia on the Gulf of Salerno. This city was to remain completely Greek—historically, traditionally, culturally—for more than two centuries, until, in the fifth century B.C., fell to the neighboring Lucanians, who renamed it Paestum. These Lucanians, Italic tribesmen from the mountains of the nearby interior, ruled Paestum until 273 B.C., when the city fell under Roman domination.

So much for the strict historical background. In 1967, at the behest of the Italian government's Office of Antiquities in Salerno, I began to direct the excavation of the necropolises outside Paestum. From the outset our efforts yielded results beyond our expectations, but the most electrifying discovery of all came in the summer of 1968: a tomb dating from early in the fifth century B.C., the stone slab walls of which were covered with frescoes! These wall paintings were unmistakably Greek, and the tomb that they decorated soon became known, after the view of a diving man on one of its panels (see pages 26–27), as the Diver's Tomb.

At the funeral banquet in the Diver's Tomb (top) all the diners are men, in accordance with the Greek custom. This appears to rule out Etruscan authorship, for Etruscan women dined with men, sharing a couch as in the sarcophagus sculpture just above.

Hardly less exciting was the discovery in 1969 of a necropolis from the second half of the fourth century B.C. Almost half of its tombs were formed of stone slabs; they contained not only painted vases, figured terra-cottas, gold and silver jewels, and incised precious stones but also—and herein lies the originality of the find—approximately two hundred slabs covered with frescoes.

Thus, two successive finds added two new chapters to the history of ancient Greek culture in its two main stages, Classical and Hellenistic.

The painted slabs in the Diver's Tomb can be dated with confidence to about 480 B.C. This dating is based on objects in the tomb and on such stylistic details as the manner of rendering eyes and abdominal muscles and the forms of the vases shown. The paintings resemble, moreover, those on pottery of the same period.

So the Diver's Tomb frescoes were painted at a time when Paestum was completely Greek. In 480 B.C. the so-called Temple of Ceres had just been finished, and the so-called Temple of Neptune (which is, in a sense, the most Greek of all Greek monuments) had not yet been built. Clearly, no art could then have flourished in Paestum that was not essentially Greek.

A closer look at the Diver's Tomb frescoes serves to dispel any lingering doubts of their Greek origin. Their leading characteristic is their total compositional balance. Individual figures are, moreover, imbued with monumentality. All this is Greek and only Greek. Then, too, the draftsmanship is so sure, and the detachment of the figures from the background so deftly done, that these frescoes could only be the expression of an art that had attained a very high level.

But let us suppose, for a moment, that these paintings were not Greek. What other art could have produced them? Etruscan painting leaps to mind, but a comparison of the Diver's Tomb frescoes with the finest Etruscan paintings reveals big differences. The drawing underlying Etruscan paintings is slighter, more nervous, and very often less accurate, while the figures, though full of movement, lack monumentality. In Etruscan painting, moreover, the composition tends to be diffuse and

fragmented, with none of the coherence and the strict unity that characterize the Greek artistic vision—and the paintings of the Diver's Tomb.

At first glance these frescoes may appear Etruscan from their subjects. In the Diver's Tomb a funeral banquet is shown with guests reclining on tricliniums, intent on love play and music. The theme is, indeed, common in Etruscan painting. Looking closer, however, we find substantial differences: the banquet guests are male lovers (which is typically Greek), whereas in Etruscan paintings the encounters are always between persons of opposite sexes.

The conclusions to be drawn from the Diver's Tomb frescoes are clear, but the paintings discovered in 1969 are another matter. They all date from between 320 and 340 B.C. In them are hunting scenes, bloody fights between foot soldiers, chariot races, mounted horsemen, flautists, weeping women, flowered garlands and wreaths, boxing matches, mules pulling little chariots, and numerous satirical and comic scenes.

These paintings are classified as Lucanian, but this simply means that they were painted when Paestum was under Lucanian rule. The question remains: were they produced by a culture that was still Greek or by one that could be called Lucanian?

This question must be answered with caution, the more so since these pictures display a tremendous variety of artistic approaches. In some, the artist is repeating themes from earlier times and could therefore be called a traditionalist; in others, new features appear, such as depth, the sense of space, a rapid and convulsive movement of the scene. These new features are characteristic of Greek art of the second half of the fourth century B.C., so whoever painted *these* pictures could be called a modernist.

In some of the paintings the artist is obviously unsophisticated, but is striving to imitate Greek models. Though not a Greek himself, he is trying to paint in accordance with a Greek lesson, which he has, however, learned very badly. Certain other paintings are "ungrammatical"—primitive but amusing—and whoever painted these slabs was not only not a Greek but also quite unaware of Greek artistic culture.

So those paintings from the fourth century B.C. that are customarily called Lucanian are, indeed, in part Lucanian, that is, crude and ingenuous; but they are also, in part, Greek. Painted in the very years when Alexander the Great was carving out his Eastern empire, they vividly reveal the heightened use of color, the looser composition, and the exploratory mixing of styles that were to characterize Hellenistic art.

Mario Napoli, of the University of Salerno and the Paestum Museum, is Superintendent of Antiquities for Salerno and the author of books on Magna Graecia.

Painted about 480 years before Christ's birth, this daring young man has been flying through the air for almost two and a half millenniums. He appears on the inside of the slab that covered the sarcophagus known, for him, as the Diver's Tomb. The rendering of his eye and muscles help to date the painting and confirm its authorship as Greek.

This diving scene is unusual, perhaps unique, but other scenes pictured in the Diver's Tomb, such as the funeral banquet shown on the two preceding pages, occur, too, on Greek vases of the period. Their sure draftsmanship and balanced composition, moreover, and the monumentality of the human figures they depict, also stamp them as Greek.

The influence of the Greeks can be seen in the sophisticated modeling of the horses in this scene from the Child's Tomb (340–320 B.C.), which presumably portrays one of the contestants in a four-in-hand chariot race.

In this busy scene from the Black Horse Tomb, a griffonlike beast (at left) looks on as two armed men engage in what may be a mock skirmish, a musician plays his flute, and two women seemingly carry out mourning rites.

Though the soldier opposite was painted on a wall of the Monumental Chariot Tomb almost a full century after Paestum fell to the Lucanians, his helmet, beard, and bearing remain Greek. The wall paintings of the so-called Lucanian era, done at the very start of the Hellenistic age, are a fascinating blend of classical Greek and livelier, less formal, local styles.

DESIGNER
IN THE
DESERT

Architect Soleri sketches one of his visionary cities.

In his Arizona "earth colony"
Paolo Soleri dreams up structures
that are really
cities for millions of people

An exhibition hall of dramatic, cavelike aspect is one of the several earth and

concrete buildings that form Soleri's homemade desert workshop. A gathering place for Soleri's disciples, it is located not far from Scottsdale, Arizona.

Modern man in his technical prowess faces three unnerving trends. First, the world population is increasing rapidly. Secondly, the proportion of people living in cities is rising rapidly. Thirdly, and in consequence, spreading cities and suburbs now coalesce with neighboring cities and suburbs to form blighting megalopolises over alarmingly large stretches of the earth. We are approaching the time when the old debate about city life versus country life will have become obsolete, for the great majority of people will have neither, but rather, something inferior to both.

The grand question, obviously, is what can we do about it? Without evading the basic facts (the population is not going to shrink or return to the farm), what is the best we can *imagine* doing about it?

The latter question is far more difficult than it may seem. To conceive of ideal living conditions for hundreds of millions of people, to design the shape and inner structure of ideal possible cities, calls for a titanic exercise of imagination and intellect, and for encyclopedic knowledge. Fortunately, men of the requisite imagination and boldness do exist, and one such visionary planner is Paolo Soleri, a gifted Italian-born architect who has spent years of obscurity in the Arizona desert, drafting, in his words, "guidelines toward a new option" for modern man, the city dweller.

To Soleri, the great problem of urbanization is not that more and more people will be living in hideously cramped and overcrowded cities. In his view we suffer from the opposite defect: our cities are not compressed enough. Existing cities are so little capable of concentrating urban activities within their proper sphere that parts of the urban environment must be flung out onto the surrounding countryside if they are to be accommodated.

Yet cities once contained fairly adequately all the people and activities they brought together. Because they did so, cities had definite boundaries, beyond which lay an uncontaminated countryside within easy reach and capable of being enjoyed by the city dwellers. It is Soleri's ultimate premise that modern technology makes it feasible for cities to be this way again, and for the countryside to be accessible to urban dwellers once more. What is required to achieve this is a grasp of what is possible.

For Soleri, two related principles open up new possibilities for urban man. These he calls "complexity" and "miniaturization," although the terms "intricacy" and "compression" are perhaps more descriptive. In Soleri's visionary cities populations are enormously concentrated within small areas by a variety of technical means, their forms arranged so that urban functions are tightly co-ordinated and interwoven organs of the city do double and triple duty—habitations, for example, serving as parts of a transportation network. Most important, Soleri's cities are fully three-dimensional environments, "not a thin pancake," as he says, but elaborately multileveled structures.

What makes this drastic compression possible—and all Soleri's cities can be viewed as experiments in compression—is that each city is designed as a single, unified, and continuous structure, with a remarkable variety of forms combined to increase the compactness of the whole and make the fullest possible use of the vertical, or third dimension. They are buildings that function like metropolises; metropolises in the form of buildings.

Architectural design on such a gigantic scale is scarcely what we think of when we use the term "architecture." Soleri himself calls his cities "arcologies," a word he coined by amalgamating "architecture" and "ecology," the former suggesting the aspect of unified structural design, the latter that what is being designed is nothing less than basic patterns of life for vast populations—new human ecologies.

What has Soleri accomplished with his visionary arcologies? There is no simple answer. Soleri himself is so sure that others' visions will surpass his own that he refers to his city plans as "Model T's"—they may dazzle contemporaries, but they will one day appear quaintly antiquated. "What you see," he has said of his cities, "is a phantom, the beginning of a process." On the other hand, he is convinced that those who come after him must follow the rules of "complexity and miniaturization," which Soleri sees as parts of a general evolutionary pattern manifest throughout the history of organic life. In short, other urban designers will design superior cities, but the cities will be in the form of vast three-dimensional structures.

Soleri's faith in the evolutionary soundness of his principles is, to a degree, a source of weakness. Although he calls his designs cities "in the image of man," they seem too often to be cities in the image of his principles—fleshings out of the notion of "complexity," applications of the notion of "miniaturization." It may well be that men would prefer to exchange a small amount of suburban sprawl for a little less compression.

No man can give due weight to all human considerations, of course, which is why every utopia ever described looks a little sparse. Yet compared with the kind of urban designer who would "solve" the problem of crowding by building secondary cities on top of already existing ones, Soleri has offered new options that are truly new and truly options. This is no small achievement, for what he has done is make a clear-cut addition to man's stock of imaginings, a stock that is always in need of replenishment and without which we can make no new beginnings at all.

By WALTER KARP

SOLERI'S ARCOLOGIES

HEXAHEDRON

A city on stilts, "Hexahedron" is a Soleri arcology so fully three-dimensional that to speak of its population density per square mile (forty-six times that of Chicago) would be meaningless. As shown in Soleri's scale model, left, and drawing, below, Hexahedron consists chiefly of two three-sided pyramids, one of them with its apex facing earthward. The city center is the vertical core of the megastructure, which means that every resident of the city is within half a mile of the downtown facilities— a supreme virtue of compression in Soleri's view. An outline of the Empire State Building indicates the scale.

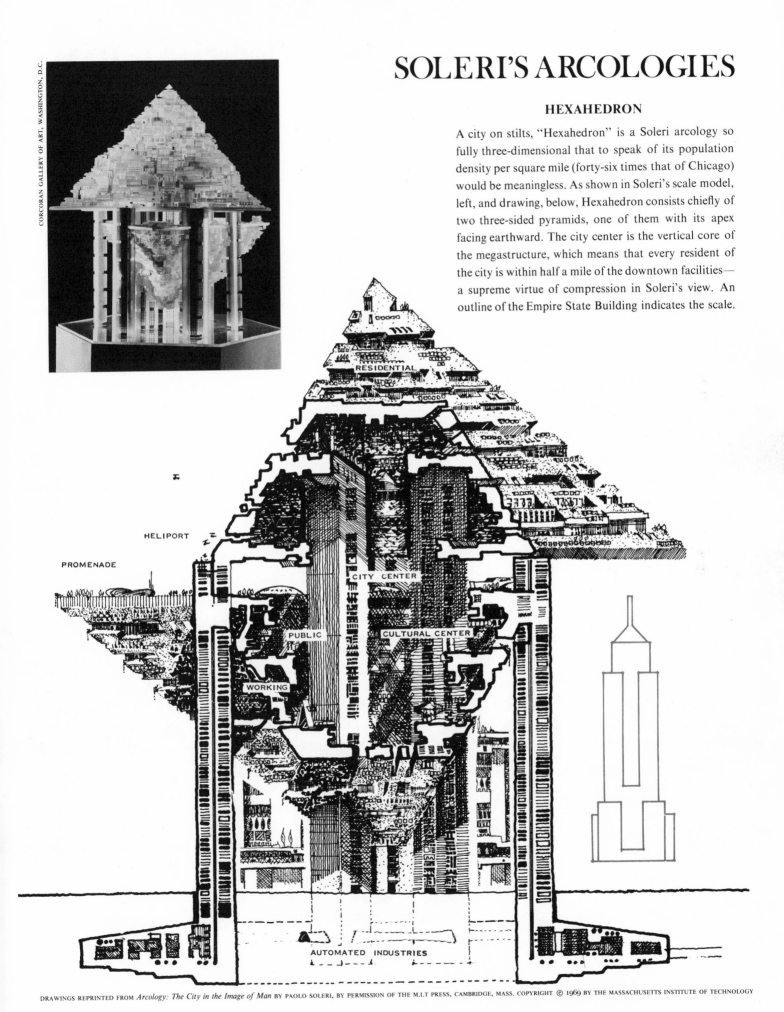

RESIDENTIAL

HELIPORT

PROMENADE

CITY CENTER

PUBLIC

CULTURAL CENTER

WORKING

AUTOMATED INDUSTRIES

DRAWINGS REPRINTED FROM *Arcology: The City in the Image of Man* BY PAOLO SOLERI, BY PERMISSION OF THE M.I.T PRESS, CAMBRIDGE, MASS. COPYRIGHT © 1969 BY THE MASSACHUSETTS INSTITUTE OF TECHNOLOGY

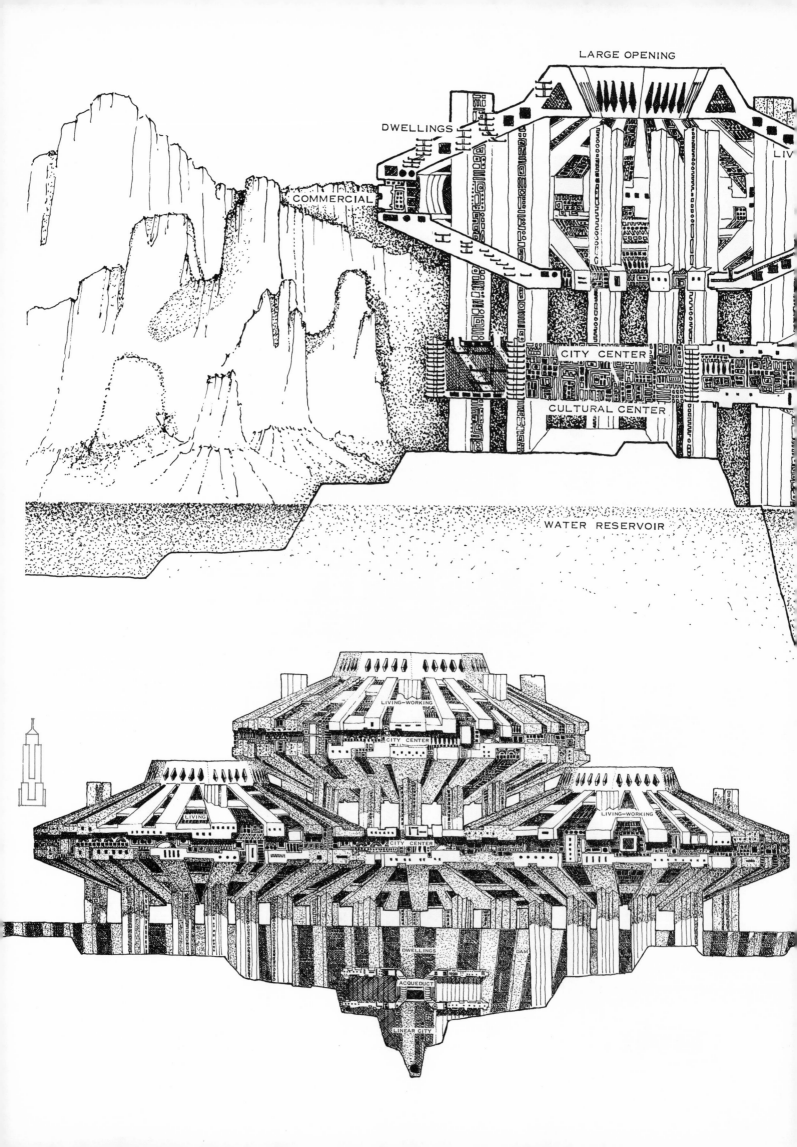

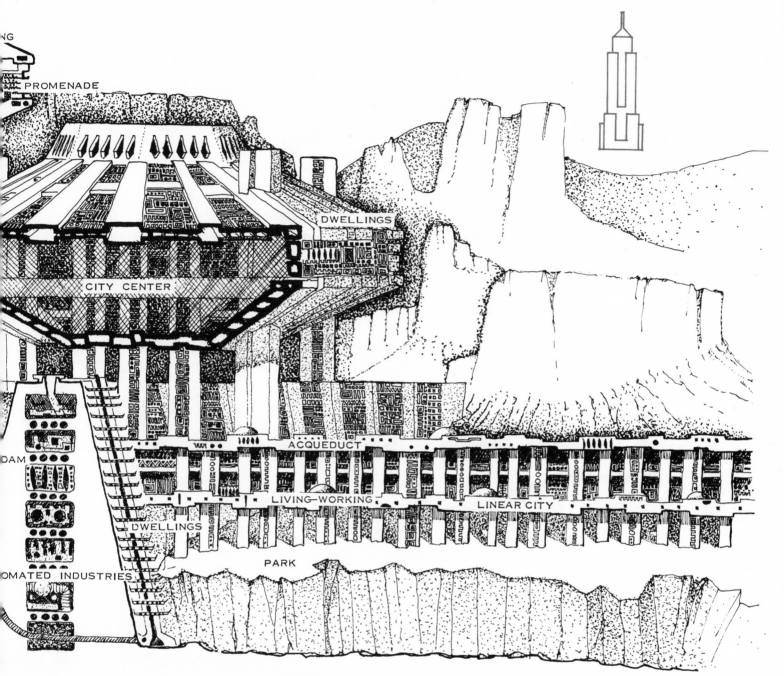

NG

PROMENADE

DWELLINGS

CITY CENTER

DAM

ACQUEDUCT

DWELLINGS

LIVING-WORKING

LINEAR CITY

OMATED INDUSTRIES

PARK

BABELDIGA

A city that serves as a dam, "Babeldiga" not only supplies its own power but houses more than a million people in a structure that measures over a mile from its underground base to its cliff-level top. Although the urban environment of Babeldiga is largely "indoors," as shown in the sketch opposite of the whole city, its residents would live primarily on the outer surface of the structure. They would thus face outward toward an unsullied environment— Soleri's cities have no suburbs—as well as inward toward an environment as artificial as that of a city on the moon. In his arcological designs, Soleri has labeled general areas of activity but has left the details unspecified. Again outlines of the Empire State Building indicate scale.

BABEL II D

A city contained within a tower, right, "Babel II D" is more than a mile high and can accommodate over half a million inhabitants. It is not, however, merely a grotesquely oversize apartment-house with layer upon narrow layer of residential "flats." Each story of Babel II D ("Babel" is Soleri's generic name for several tower-like cities that he has designed) is a circular platform supporting an entire neighborhood complete with streets and residences.

LIGHT WELL

NEIGHBORHOOD

COMMERCIAL

PUBLIC

PARK   PROMENADE

CITY CENTER   LIVING

PUBLIC

WORKING   DWELLINGS

WAREHOUSING

AUTOMATED INDUSTRIES   FACTORIES AND UTILITIES

NOVANOAH I

A latter-day Noah's Ark, as its name implies, "Nova-noah I," at right, is Soleri's plan for a floating city of some four hundred thousand people. The top diagram presents a view of the circumference of the circular man-made island, the lower a cross section of its center. "A rounded microcosmos and not a thin pancake," Nova-noah I, like all Soleri's arcologies, is an elaborately multileveled city in which elevators and escalators become the basic means of transportation. The "extracting and harvesting industries," shown in the lower diagram, would draw in foodstuffs and raw materials from the sea.

BUOYANT STRUCTURE

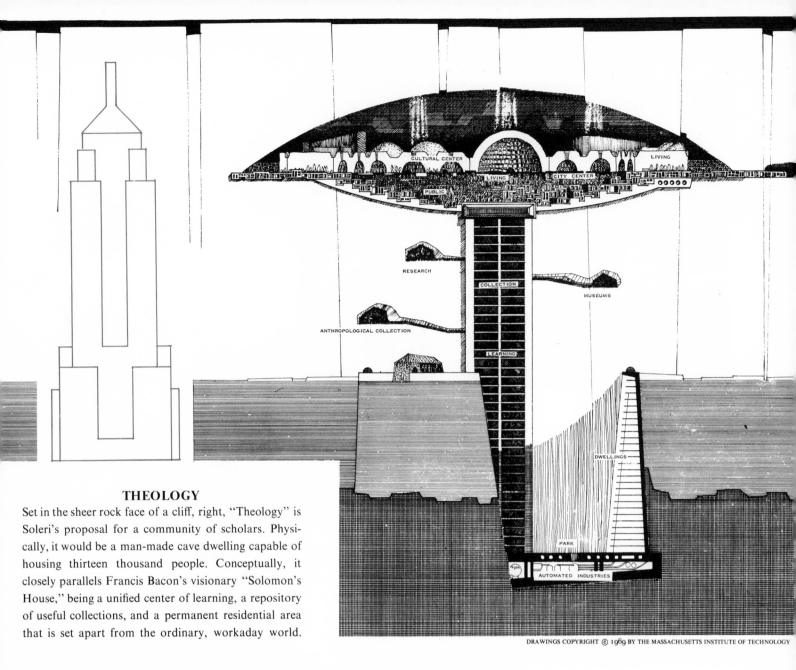

THEOLOGY

Set in the sheer rock face of a cliff, right, "Theology" is Soleri's proposal for a community of scholars. Physically, it would be a man-made cave dwelling capable of housing thirteen thousand people. Conceptually, it closely parallels Francis Bacon's visionary "Solomon's House," being a unified center of learning, a repository of useful collections, and a permanent residential area that is set apart from the ordinary, workaday world.

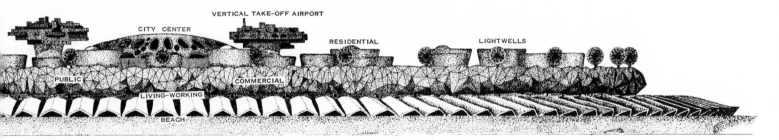

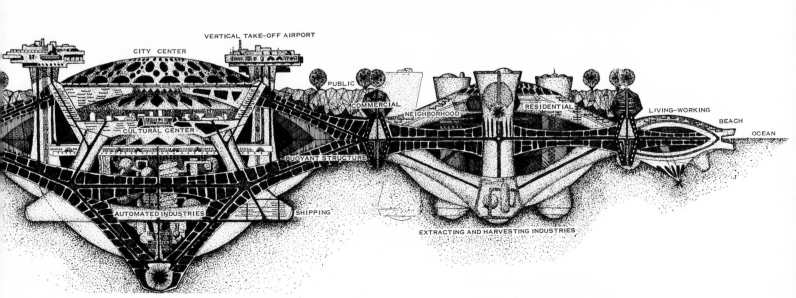

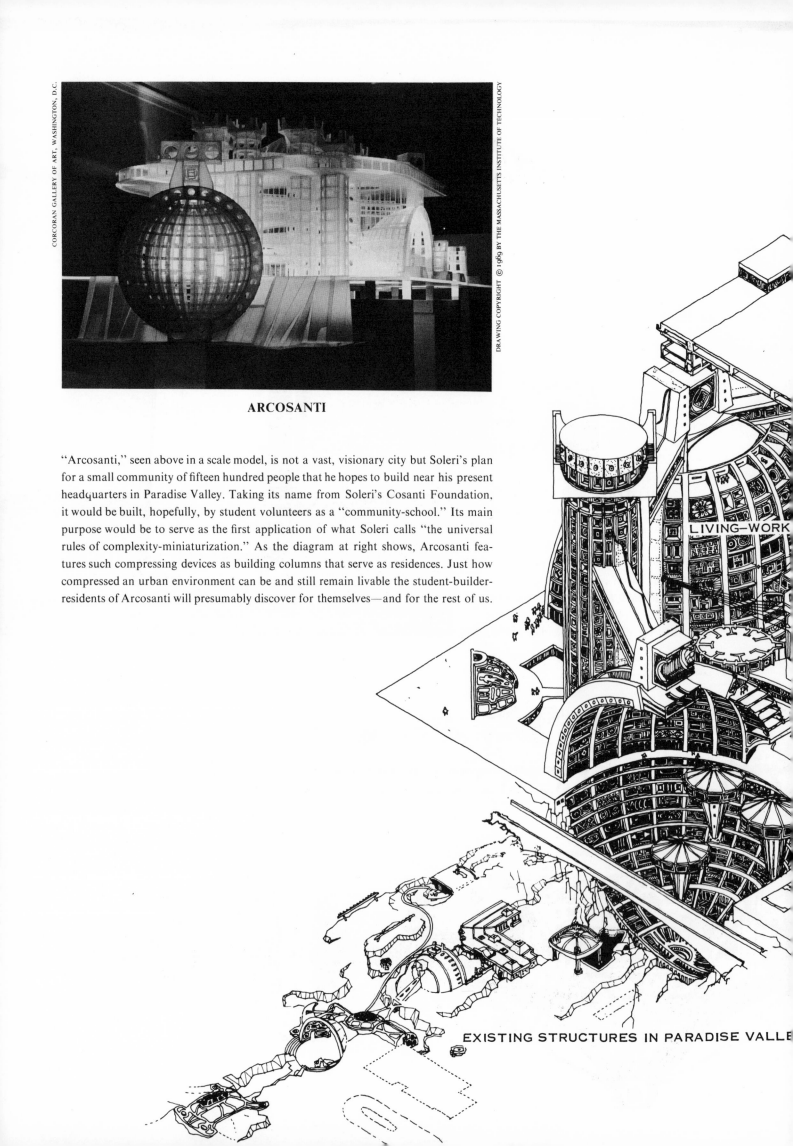

ARCOSANTI

"Arcosanti," seen above in a scale model, is not a vast, visionary city but Soleri's plan for a small community of fifteen hundred people that he hopes to build near his present headquarters in Paradise Valley. Taking its name from Soleri's Cosanti Foundation, it would be built, hopefully, by student volunteers as a "community-school." Its main purpose would be to serve as the first application of what Soleri calls "the universal rules of complexity-miniaturization." As the diagram at right shows, Arcosanti features such compressing devices as building columns that serve as residences. Just how compressed an urban environment can be and still remain livable the student-builder-residents of Arcosanti will presumably discover for themselves—and for the rest of us.

LIVING–WORK

EXISTING STRUCTURES IN PARADISE VALLE

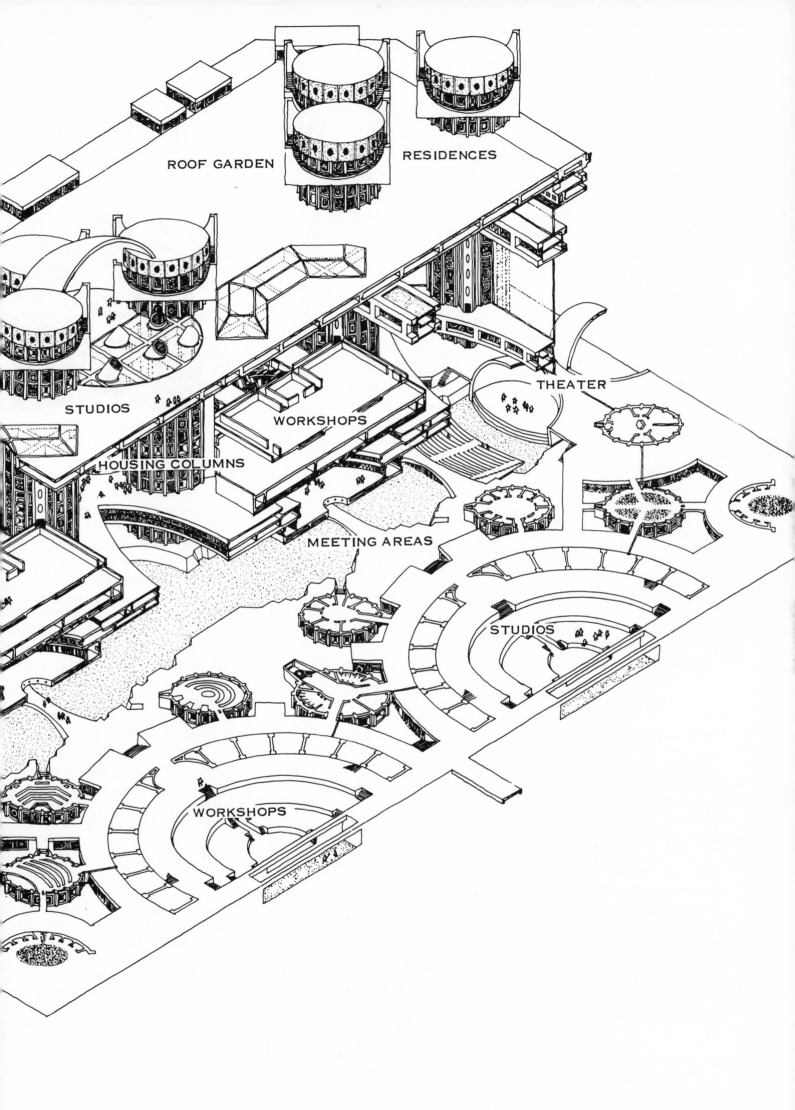

ROOF GARDEN

RESIDENCES

STUDIOS

HOUSING COLUMNS

WORKSHOPS

THEATER

MEETING AREAS

STUDIOS

WORKSHOPS

By J. H. PLUMB

WERE THEY RIGHT?

There they were on a Sunday morning in the 1890's, pedaling with determination along the New Jersey Palisades until they found a quiet stretch of river. Then they stripped off their serviceable knickerbockers and blouses, and bathed, glowing with high-minded morality, quite naked. Refreshed, they sat down to a healthy picnic of wholemeal bread, raw carrots, fruit, and nuts. They sang a few glees, danced to "Gathering Peascods" or "Jack's Mag-

Strenuous living: a troop of alpine climbers

got," mounted their bicycles, and full of virtue, pedaled back to the ferry for New York.

Men might scoff and women might scorn, but they were the avant-garde, the pioneers of a better life, the leaders of the new way, the social reformers who by the shining example of their lives would help to dispel the moral squalor, the filth, the commercialization, and the sadism of their day.

Across the Atlantic, similar knots of men and women were hiking across the Chilterns or pedaling along the dusty roads of the Kentish downs. The men wore sensible clothing—tweed plus fours, open-necked shirts, straw boaters. Some of the women might be hatless; all, except the youngest, were shapeless, for they disapproved of gir-

dles, corsets, bustles, and the like. They were clothing reformers, pacifists, vegetarians, nudists; they made pots, carved wood, wove on handlooms, played recorders, did folk dances, supported civil liberties, voted socialist, opposed child labor, advocated birth control, cultivated Gypsies, explored Celtic mythology, abhorred churches, and attended séances. They were free with children and gentle to animals; they hated fox hunters, loathed fur, and despised feathered headdresses— indeed, they organized a protest movement to stop the use of birds' feathers for clothing. Wood fires, cold baths, wide-open bedroom windows, Japanese prints, Gothic furniture, and Morris chintz adorned their homes. On their bookshelves could be found Thoreau, Ruskin, Whitman, Morris, W. H. Hudson, Shaw, Wells, and the Webbs. The more adventurous had taken up camping, canoeing, and mountaineering in order to get closer to nature, which for most of them had replaced the anthropomorphic God.

These were the faddists. Of course, they were not uniform. Some ate meat, some eschewed eggs and milk as a violation of natural diet, many would not under any circumstances eat cooked food or drink anything but water. Some married, others refused to do so;

Natural living: graceful bliss beside a lake

Feminism: a clutch of resolute suffragettes

some went nude and others would not. Most of the women were feminists, and their men supported them. Most of the men were pacifists and socialists, and their women supported them. They all belonged to dedicated societies for social protest or amelioration. Intelligentsia, Bohemians, faddists, or cranks, call them what you will, they are the spiritual grandparents of our children. They were numerous enough to catch the public eye and to be pilloried by the satirists of *Punch*. Yet, they could be, and were, ignored or dismissed as fools and self-important prigs. The men of authority assumed that they were wrongheaded, at best eccentric, at worst anarchistic, but always a ripe target for reactionary abuse. And yet, were they wrong?

Wherever one looks in late Victorian or Edwardian England, and the same is true of America, one finds small bands of dedicated men and women, usually of upper-middle-class origin—but sometimes joined by bank clerks, insurance agents, and skilled artisans—who had come together to reform the life that they detested. A typical society in England was the Fellowship of the New Life, founded by Thomas Davidson in the 1880's, whose members believed passionately in fraternity, open air, sensible clothing, folk pastimes, and freedom of thought and were intensely suspicious of commercial and industrial society, which they felt destroyed life's harmonies, devastated the countryside, and contaminated food, all for the sake of profit and grab. It was in this fellowship that Havelock Ellis met Edward Carpenter, who preached the virtues and naturalness of homosexual love before, and after, Oscar Wilde was clapped into jail. This same fellowship spawned the tough-minded Fabians, whose incisive criticism of society created the intellectual bone structure of the English socialist movement. These men and women reacted violently *against* their society, giving their enthusiasm to myriad causes that their own world thought screwball.

John Galsworthy, the novelist, belonged to the stuffier upper-middle class by origin, but his sensitivity, his intelligence, and his deep sense of moral obligation drove him toward Bohemia. The causes that he supported from time to time give a fascinating insight into the huge constellation of faddist and do-gooder societies of our great-grandparents, ranging as they do from politics to the protection of birds. They were: "abolition of the censorship of plays, sweated industries, minimum wage, labour unrest, labour exchanges, woman's suffrage, ponies in mines, divorce law reform, prison reform . . . aeroplanes in war, docking of horses' tails, for love of beasts, slaughterhouse reform, plumage bill, caging of wild birds, worn-out horse traffic, performing animals, vivisection of dogs, dental experiments on dogs, pigeon shooting, slum clearance, zoos, Cecil

Outdoor exercise: a cyclist in pedal pushers

houses, children on the stage, the three year average income tax."

Much that Galsworthy and his allies fought for has been won. Cats are no longer skinned alive for fun in the streets of London and New York. Children cannot be beaten insensible by their fathers with impunity. Women no longer wear stuffed birds on their hats: birds and beasts are protected. Wives are no longer slaves. Sex is no longer a shameful word. All these things are *their* victories, the result of their bravery in withstanding social ostracism, harassment by police, sometimes, as with Carpenter and Ellis, prosecution. Social disapproval did not deter them. They were right, overwhelmingly right —sometimes for the wrong reasons, sometimes for the right ones—but their suspicion of science, of the more artificial aspects of modern living, of the exploitation of women, children, and animals, was utterly sound, and as we know to our cost, many of their battles are far from over.

Kindliness: two dray horses with sunbonnets

But our modern protest groups rarely realize that they are the heirs of a long tradition, just as many of the late Victorians and Edwardians were ignorant of those who had protested long before them. Concern about the treatment of children began in the eighteenth century; societies to protect animals from human cruelty were established in England by 1824. Food reformers were active before 1850, especially in America, where Sylvester Graham preached the virtues of whole-meal flour in the 1830's and crusaded against the eating of meat. Amelia Bloomer was crusading for clothing reform in America by the middle of the century. And the back-to-nature cult had its apostles even before Thoreau and Ruskin. But these

Athleticism: a pole-vaulting Nebraska coed

early voices had been lonely: they were rarely institutionalized in clubs, societies, or fellowships until about the 1880's, when the faddists became a social, if not a political, force. Since then, their reputations have fluctuated, but increasingly, as we discern the violence we have done to our environment, the pollution in which we have drenched ourselves, and the crippling effect modern society has had on our emotional lives, we realize that these men and women were not cranks, not faddists, not screwballs, but that they were right.

41

WHOSE SATYRICON
—Petronius's or Fellini's?

The director, says our classical scholar, has mined the
original to create his own *brutto spettacolo* of a pagan
world—as it was in Nero's time, and as it may be in ours

By GILBERT HIGHET

In his film adaptation of Petronius's
*Satyricon** Federico Fellini has created
a memorable world of imagination.
One of his reviewers compared it to
an adult Land of Oz—not inappropri-
ately, for his figures and scenery appear to exist in some other dimension,
which can be entered only through the
doors of hallucination. A gigantic slum
tenement crumbling into earthquake-
shattered fragments; a dark subterranean bath-establishment full of vaults
and tunnels; a nightmare slave-ship,
black and misshapen—these and a
dozen other spectacles are so strange,
and are presented with such clarity by
the camera, that they are impossible to
forget. The ordered sanity of the filmed
Julius Caesar, the simple good-and-bad
opposition of *Quo Vadis?,* have no
place here. It is a real shock, right in
the middle of the picture, to be shown
a quiet, ordinary home inhabited by a
handsome and perfectly sane lady and
gentleman, with flowers and birds and
running water and civilized manners.
But even that home is doomed: the husband—apparently modeled on Thrasea
Paetus—frees his slaves and kills himself, followed by his wife. Normal
people cannot live in such a world.

*I believe it ought to be *Satyrica,* like Virgil's *Georgica*
and Manilius's *Astronomica,* but the other form is apparently established now.

*Federico Fellini shows an actor how to play
the role of Vernacchio, a depraved Roman
actor, in his film version of the* Satyricon.

Most motion pictures laid in ancient
times err by making everyone too
straightforward and too modern: Sam-
son is played by Victor Mature, clean-
shaven and handsome, without a hair
on his chest or armpits; King Arthur,
or Henry VIII, or Mark Antony, they
all look and talk like Richard Burton,
and they are surrounded by ordinary
men and women in costume. But Fellini's *Satyricon* is full of abnormal peo-

ple. A deformed dwarf; a hermaphrodite; an immensely fat woman, half-
naked; an ancient hook-nosed crone,
bewigged, lipsticked, and chalk-pow-
dered; a maniac tied hand and foot;
they bewilder and horrify the onlooker
like the visions of Pieter Bruegel.

In a chapter of his book on World
War II, *Kaputt,†* Curzio Malaparte describes how, after being released from
prison in 1943, he returned to Naples
at the beginning of an air raid. To escape the bombs, the populace dived
into an underground city formed by
grottoes and galleries excavated in the
Middle Ages. They were followed by a
mob of apparitions more terrifying
than the bombs: the cripples, the deformed, the monsters who in normal
times are kept hidden away by pity,
horror, superstition, or family shame—
skeletons clothed in rags, old men with
dog faces, children with apelike features. They were led by a monarch too
dreadful to be seen, a deity shrouded
head to foot in a silken coverlet
and supported by a group of hideous
dwarfs. Slowly, in a sinister silence
broken only by a woman's prayer or
a child's scream, this procession, like
an army of demons returning to hell,
entered a cavern and disappeared.

†Translated by C. Foligno (Dutton, 1946).

Fellini's Trimalchio, opposite, re-creates a parvenu ex-slave, displaying his wealth with a garish feast.

To such a world belong most of the people of Fellini's *Satyricon.* Even when they are normally built, they are masked, or grotesquely painted and ornamented, or else they look ill or drunk or perverted. There is a strong, brutal sea-captain, healthy and vigorous—except that he has one dead, glaring eye. There is a Negro witch, played by Donyale Luna, who is immensely tall and immensely thin, a Masai princess. Apart from Thrasea Paetus and his wife, and their servants, the only normal-looking people I can remember are Encolpius, the strikingly handsome young hero, and Ascyltus, his jaunty young foil, part Iago, part Mephistopheles. There are one or two beautiful women, overdressed and heavily made up—although in Petronius's *Satyricon,* one of the finest episodes concerns a girl too lovely for the hero to describe, with starbright eyes and a mouth like Diana's. Most of the characters in Fellini would be at home in *The Cabinet of Dr. Caligari.*

With some reservations, I believe this is good cinema. The world of Petronius is wild. Reading the narrative, you are often stimulated but often shocked. The hero and his companions hurry from one painful adventure to another. Now they dine with a millionaire whose manners and guests are so vulgar that, first amused and then revolted, they seize the earliest chance to escape. Now they wander into a red-light district, and they are beset by whores and pederasts. Now they take ship, find that the captain is a deadly enemy, and (worst of indignities) disguise themselves as runaway slaves, shaved and branded. When Encolpius gets a pretty and loving girl on a bed of flowers, he becomes impotent. He quarrels with his companion about a young catamite, and tries to hang himself. In other parts of the satire that are now lost, the two heroes, or antiheroes, apparently had equally agonizing trials: one or another of them appeared as a thief, as a scapegoat doomed to be cast aside after a year's high living, as a gladiator vowed to death.

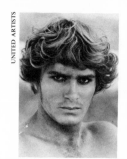

Roman male beauty: left, Fellini's Encolpius; right, Hadrian's favorite, Antinous.

Since we have only fragments of the original book, no one can reconstruct the main plot with any certainty. But it looks as though it were a parody both of the love-romances, such as Heliodorus's *Aethiopica,* and of Homer's *Odyssey.* The love is not the pure affection of a man and a woman separated by ill fortune, but the disreputable amours of homosexuals and adulterers; and the hero is not a clever prince pursued by the anger of the sea-god Poseidon, but a phenomenally endowed sexual athlete pursued by the anger of the sex-god Priapus. If this, or something like it, is true, then Petronius's *Satyricon* is a bizarre fantasy. It is at the same time more brutally realistic and more grotesquely fanciful than any classical work now extant. Its author has a marvelous ear for low conversation and a wild experience of low life. Other men must have had the second, if not the first; but only one of them has left a comparable book, the *Metamorphoses* of Apuleius, and that, although full of vile and cruel adventures, is far less realistic in style.

When the young emperor Nero was nineteen, he developed the habit of going out slumming. Disguised, he visited bars and brothels and mean streets. He and his companions robbed shops and insulted passers-by, until one night he himself got into a fight and was beaten. Once, long ago, I suggested that Petronius—who was an intimate friend of Nero, and his "arbiter of taste"—wrote the *Satyricon* partly to amuse him, and partly to educate him in the Epicurean manner by showing him how miserable, ridiculous, and dangerous such a roving life actually can be.* Of course it is impossible to

*"Petronius the Moralist," *Transactions of the American Philological Association* (1941).

prove this; yet the book certainly gives a powerful impression of the squalors and miseries endured by homeless wanderers without careers or trades or cash, with dirty pasts and dangerous futures. To match this, Fellini gives us a suitably phantasmagoric story line, jumping from one episode to another with little attention to logical sequence.

Mind you, speaking as a classicist, I thought most of the scenery was painfully improbable. The sinister slave-ship could not have sailed ten miles in a strong Mediterranean breeze. The gladiatorial duel did not take place in a proper arena, but in a sand pit without seats or gates, which is like putting a baseball game out in the Jersey swamps. Roman baths in the period of the empire were brilliantly lit and sumptuously decorated; Fellini's baths look like the catacombs or Piranesi ruins. And so on. Yet all these scenes possess a nightmarish vividness.

So much for the characters and scenery. What has Fellini done with the story? The original *Satyricon* of Petronius got through the Dark Ages only in torn and battered copies full of gaps. Sometimes only one sentence survived out of a whole chapter. The beginning is gone. The end is gone. The continuity is lost. We do not even know how long the tale was. A note in one manuscript implies that the millionaire's banquet was Book Fifteen. Now, it runs to over fifty pages. If there were twenty such books, the whole thing would be better than a thousand of our pages, a giant half as long as Proust. (The serious Greek love-romances are pretty long, too, but do not contain so wide a variety of characters and speeches.) Fellini had the problem of making a continuous work of art out of a scarred, fragmentary torso with its head and limbs knocked off. This he has done very well. Encolpius, the anti-hero, with his vicious associates, is projected onto the screen in the first minute; their adventures link on to one another illogically but grippingly; and at the end they suddenly fade away, like modern motorcycle gypsies, into the distance.

The story, however, has been greatly changed. Fellini has introduced many new characters and incidents, has altered many episodes and borrowed some scenes from other sources. He is more than an interpreter of Petronius. He is a competitor. He is a creator. It would take considerable research to trace the sources of all Fellini's innovations, but some can be explained.

Early in the book we see Encolpius and his companions penniless, living in a slum. Petronius says little of its appearance or its inhabitants. But Fellini builds it into an enormous tenement block, populates it with a horde of loathsome men and women, and then has it tremble, sag, and collapse in an earthquake. I believe he thought of this because of the earthquake that partly destroyed Pompeii in Nero's time, and because the satirist Juvenal says:

Our city is propped up by fragile timbers,
or most of it. Landlords postpone collapse
by shoring up, and plastering over the
   cracks—
telling us to sleep sound in the tottering
   ruin.*

Later on the anti-hero, afflicted by temporary impotence, visits an old drunken witch, miserably poor, called Oenothea (Wine-goddess), and is cured. In the film, Oenothea becomes a Negro sorceress, young and handsome in a weird, exotic way. But a flashback gives us some of her history. A wizard once loved her. She humiliated him. He cast a spell that put out all the fires in the vicinity and told the neighbors they could only kindle their fires at her private parts. And so they come in, each with his bit of kindling, and Oenothea is degraded, and the fire catches, and she screams, and his revenge is complete. This is not a classical story at all: it is a medieval tale, and the obscene part of it is Oriental in origin. In the Middle Ages it was told about Virgil (then conceived of not as a poet but as a magician).† It is difficult to see what it is doing here, especially since it concerns a subordinate character. Except

this: Fellini enjoys showing women lying down and being sexually degraded in public. Petronius does not.

Fellini invents another scene in which a writhing nymphomaniac gets temporary satisfaction from Encolpius and his friend in the presence of her husband; and still another, the most evilly fantastic, in which the hero, after fighting a gladiator dressed as the Minotaur in a labyrinth, is supposed to be Theseus, wins the princess Ariadne, and is expected to possess her before a large audience. Of course he fails, and she is furious. Fellini got this idea, I believe, from Suetonius's biography of Nero, where he says that the degenerate young emperor showed a bull mounting a wooden cow supposedly containing Queen Pasiphae (as in the Cretan legend) "so that many of the spectators believed it." But Fellini's scene is cruder and more realistic. Nor does Ariadne look like the pretty young Minoan princess who helped Theseus return from the mortal maze, but enough like a blasé Egyptian courtesan to repel even a youngster who had not just been fighting for his life.‡

In another curiously repulsive episode Fellini shows a frail young bisexual creature, worshiped as the living god Hermaphrodite, being abducted by the anti-heroes and (like a victim of a modern kidnapping) dying of thirst and exhaustion during their escape. There is nothing like this in Petronius. In the time of Nero I know of no such deities embodied in human form. Much later such a cult was represented by the half-Oriental god-priest Elagabal, who became emperor in A.D. 218 at the age of fourteen and was killed by the soldiers four years later; but that was in a time of social chaos, much farther down the slope than the epoch of Nero. Petro-

nius's wandering hero did in fact commit two acts of sacrilege for which he was severely punished. He profaned the secret rites of the sex-god Priapus by witnessing them without authority, and he killed one of Priapus's sacred birds, a gander. For these offenses he had to pay humiliating penalties. Nothing of this appears in the film. Apparently Fellini sheered off from the idea that a divinity represented largely by a big male organ could be profaned and avenge itself. He chose to substitute for this a pathetic, impotent creature neither truly male nor truly female.

One further change from the original. Encolpius and his companions have an old enemy called Lichas. From certain allusions, it appears that some time ago one of them seduced his wife and insulted him. Petronius makes them board his ship, without knowing he is in command, and disguise themselves to avoid his resentment. Detected, they start a fight; but before anyone is killed, peace is made and celebrated with a drunken party. A storm follows. Captain Lichas is swept overboard and drowned. His ship is wrecked. His body is burned on the beach by the survivors, and (as they say in the Icelandic sagas) so he goes out of the story. In Petronius he is a rather simple "heavy." Fellini converts him into something more complex and sinister. In the film his ship is not a passenger vessel but a slave ship full of victims and freaks destined to amuse the emperor. He insists, after capturing Encolpius, on fighting him and humiliating him. Then he becomes a bride wearing a bridal robe and wreath, takes the dazed Encolpius as his husband, and—while the guests shout *Feliciter!* ("Good Luck!") and his own wife follows as matron of honor—proceeds simpering to a wedding chamber below decks.

In its film context this seems crazy, and very inappropriate for a tough piratic fellow such as Lichas. Apparently Fellini got the idea from the public degeneracy of the emperor Nero, who got himself married to a man

*Juvenal, *Satires*, 3.193–196.

†D. Comparetti, *Virgil in the Middle Ages,* trans. by E. F. M. Benecke (New York, 1908), explains that the fire part of the story is a legend told in a history of the Mongol khans of Turkestan that made its way westward through Byzantium. Richard Strauss transformed and ennobled the tale in his opera *Feuersnot.*

Aging matrons: left, Fellini's grotesque; right, an unknown first-century woman.

UNITED ARTISTS

LATERAN MUSEUM, ROME

‡The Roman official who presides over this affair tells Encolpius that the show is a festival honoring the god of Mirth. This notion comes from an isolated episode in the *Metamorphoses* of Apuleius (2.31 and 3.11), where the joke played on the hero is cleaner, funnier, and more imaginative.

called Pythagoras who had been a slave —except that Nero went further than Lichas. The historian Tacitus records it with tight-lipped disgust, saying, "The emperor was clad in a saffron bridal gown, there was a dowry and a marriage bed and bridal torches, everything was seen which even in a woman is concealed by night."* A generation later Juvenal the satirist tells a similar story about a corrupt nobleman of his own time, mentioning the shouts of *Feliciter!*† Yet history outdoes fiction. A little later in the film we see Lichas being seized and beheaded, his wall-eyed head floating away, gazing upward at the camera. But Tacitus, still tight-lipped, begins his next chapter with "There followed a disaster, whether due to chance or the designs of the prince . . ." and goes on to describe the great fire that destroyed much of Rome. The implication is clear.

The *Satyricon* of Petronius could be laid out as ten main blocks of action, each of them with one or more subordinate inset episodes (some mainly action sequences, others mostly speech). Fellini naturally did not try to screen two curious sections in which the disreputable old poet Eumolpus recites part of an epic on the Civil War (to cut down Petronius's contemporary Lucan) and part of a tragic description of the fall of Troy (to cut down Petronius's contemporary Seneca). Sure to stimulate discussion when read aloud at Nero's banquets, these long formal poems would be impossible in a film. Fellini also threw away most of the guests' conversation at the millionaire's banquet. In the book they chatter away, betraying their vulgarity by every sentence they utter. Most of the satirical relish is provided by their richly proliferating social, intellectual, and grammatical blunders. In the film they mainly guzzle and swill. The weight of the emphasis lies on the disgusting dishes they are offered (a whole pig, which when gutted releases not intestines but sausages, the favorite food of the lowest class of Italians) and on Trimalchio's own self-glorification.

*Tacitus, *Annals*, 15.37.8–9.
†Juvenal, *Satires*, 2.117–142.

To compensate for omitting the talk, Fellini has invented several action sequences with virtually no dialogue. A young emperor is beset and killed by soldiers, some of them wielding ten-foot-long pikes (which in fact were kept for sea battles and siege warfare, but *look* powerful). There is a glimpse of a new Caesar, stern and warlike, marching on Rome. A gigantic head of Constantine (or another very late monarch) is dragged through the streets— perhaps because Juvenal describes the head of a statue of Tiberius's fallen favorite, Sejanus, being broken up and melted down. No one who knows the history of Rome can take these little incidents seriously. The assassination of Caligula by an officer of his own guard, or Nero attempting suicide but afraid to drive the dagger home, would have been more dramatic than these sketchy scenes of immature imagination.

Knowing that both the book and the screenplay are fantasies, we do not expect historical accuracy from Fellini. But we may ask for consistency and probability within the limits of the story, and we do not always get it. Many incidents seem to be either mistakes or meaningless quirks of fancy. Take the banquet. Does Fellini really think that Romans dined lying on their stomachs? They did not. It would make anyone feel sick, particularly with so much coarse food being shoved at them. Does he really believe that, just before a dinner party in Rome, all the guests bathed naked in a swimming pool lit by scores of candles? And who on earth are the poorly dressed guests dining upstairs in a gallery, some with their backs to the host? Did Fellini misunderstand the incident in which the millionaire sends the first shift of servants away to eat supper, while a second shift comes on to attend the guests?

Perhaps. But this curious arrangement adds nothing to the dramatic value of the scene. Several other directors have the same passion for distorting an original story until it becomes almost meaningless. Buñuel's *Belle de Jour* tells the story of a scientist's pretty wife who feels neglected, takes to visiting a brothel, is at first revolted and then attracted and then corrupted and finally involved in violent gangland crime, through which her husband's life is ruined. When you see the film, you can scarcely make out whether all of this, or some of it, is merely her own erotic and masochistic fantasy. Only when you read the novel, by Joseph Kessel, do you realize that Buñuel has spoiled a clear and powerful story by infusing into it his own aberrant fantasies.

There are two central problems concerning Fellini's film. What is its relation to historical truth? And what is its relation to life in our own world today? Many people who go to see it will come away believing that the first-century Romans actually behaved like this. But to begin with, Petronius himself was writing an extravaganza such as *Candide,* a satiric exaggeration and distortion of life. Furthermore—a point that is seldom noticed—there are hardly any regular Romans in the book. Although they speak Latin, the three youths have Greek names; so do Lichas and his wife Tryphaena, and the poet Eumolpus, and the beautiful Circe, and the witch Oenothea. As for the millionaire, Trimalchio, he is from somewhere in the Near East, and his name is Semitic, from the root M-L-KH, "king"; he and his guests speak an impure Latin and are thought of as foreign parvenus. Fellini has taken Petronius's only partly Roman fantasia and has made most of it still more curious and exotic; although he did cast, or rather miscast, a modern Roman as Trimalchio, toward the end it wanders off the Italian map altogether into North Africa and Egypt. In fact, he seems not to have made up his mind whether he was composing an authen-

Roman faces: left, the evil Lichas in the Fellini film; right, a second-century Roman.

tic picture of reality—*this is how the pagan Romans lived*—or a series of surrealist visions as striking and imaginative as Goya's *Caprichos*.

He had a classicist to advise him, Luca Canali of the University of Pisa. He and his collaborator on the script, Bernardino Zapponi, visited the greatest Italian authority on Petronius, Professor Ettore Paratore, being (we are told) "a little intimidated" by his discourse. Of course they read books and visited museums. But Fellini has said several times, and I think believes, that we really *do not know* how the Romans thought and felt and lived. "It is one great nebula, full of myth . . . the atmosphere is not 'historical' but that of a dream world . . . the ancient world perhaps never existed; but we have certainly dreamed it." And yet such remarks do not explain either the energy he put into the picture, or some of his own utterances in interviews and discussions. He wants his *Satyricon* to appear as strange and forceful to us as the first Japanese film we ever saw; he even likes the assonance of *Satyricon* and *Rashomon*. In this he neglects the facts that we are closer to the ancient Romans than to the Japanese, and that the Japanese have a very keen sense for authenticity in both costume and behavior in historical dramas. But it is a misrepresentation for Fellini to suggest that the whole film is, for him, merely a psychedelic hallucination with no base in reality. He has several times remarked that the world of pagan Rome has certain analogies with our world of 1970. Therefore he must believe that we can know something about it. Rome as an ideal was (in his view) distorted by Mussolini's Fascism, which stressed its martial and organizational virtues; for these Fellini substitutes its libidinal and mystical qualities. Christianity also, he thinks, makes us misconceive paganism, for Christians see as deliberate vice what the pagans viewed as happiness and fulfillment.*

Thus, for Fellini, the *Satyricon* is not crude melodrama or pure fantasy, but a view of paganism as it was and as it

*One of the final scenes, in which Eumolpus's heirs sit gloomily eating his corpse in order to inherit his supposed wealth, may be a parody of the Last Supper; and surely the young hermaphroditic divinity that works miracles and is visited in its shrine by shepherds is a parody of the Christ child in the manger.

CAPITOLINE MUSEUM—LEONARD VON MATT   UNITED ARTISTS

The debauched Tryphaena: left, a first-century look-alike; right, her film incarnation.

will be. It is pre-Christian Rome. (Professor Santo Mazzarino reminded him that while Petronius was writing, Saint Paul was preaching; but Fellini maintained that Christian doctrine and the Christian virtues were still known only to a very few.) And it prefigures the post-Christian world that is now lurching toward its birth. The vulgar Trimalchio is a prototype of our own rich, extravagant, selfish contemporaries (Fellini's philological adviser, Canali, is said to be a Marxist). Eumolpus is the cynical and dissolute intellectual, whose keen brain and fine taste are at war with his sensual appetites. Encolpius and his two companion drifters are flower children, hippies.

Fellini admires the life-style of the hippies. He spent a whole night in a sleeping car outside Rome talking and playing with a group of them—seven girls and fifteen boys—and was delighted with the spontaneity of their emotions and thought. And the violence of the conflicts, many of them his own inventions, that punctuate the film —surely they prefigure the irrational savagery of our own era, in which kidnapping, arson, organized mob violence, and anarchic bombing threaten to supersede the orderly process of social and political life. Fellini seems to see imperial Roman society as passionate and chaotic, inhabited entirely by monsters except for two or three young, energetic, bisexual Nietzschean vagabonds. Encolpius, the best of them, is not the redeemer of this society; but, because he dodges it and uses it and derides it and evades its systematic grasp, he is its victor, not its victim.

This is a profoundly pessimistic view.

The film's pessimism comes out in the overall impression it conveys. It follows something of the same emotional pattern as *La Dolce Vita*. There, Fellini began with the flight of a helicopter over Rome (flight over a handsome city is always inspiring) and soon showed us the dazzling beauty of Anita Ekberg; but he ended with a dismal, joyless orgy and a misshapen sea-monster dying on the beach. In the same way, the *Satyricon* afflicts many spectators with disgust and world-weariness. It was surprising to watch the audience emerging from the première in Venice last year: silent, sober, with none of the usual Italian vivacity; depressed and sickened. One man spoke, to an acquaintance, one phrase: *"Brutto spettacolo!"*

The critics in France, where both the Christian church and conventional morality are taken less seriously, were unfavorably impressed. Jean Dutourd was disappointed because the promised eroticism did not appear (or rather, appeared in sinister distortions) and said he preferred *Ben-Hur*. More thoughtful, Alberto Moravia said that in spite of all his efforts, Fellini still sees pagan Rome in the same way that an early Christian would—"natural and corrupt"; and that this is why he introduces so many sick and deformed figures and so few enjoyments devoid of sinister overtones. I believe this is true. Voltaire in writing *Candide* poured scorn on the philosophical concept that this is the best of all possible worlds, but he made no judgment on ordinary life except to say that one should cultivate one's garden. Rabelais was convinced that our world *could* be the best world possible, if only . . . But Fellini thinks it is the worst of all possible worlds, endurable only through intense irresponsible pleasure followed by interminable escape. In such a world the only real people are exiles, for whom the rest of life is a *brutto spettacolo*.

The distinguished critic and classicist Gilbert Highet is a frequent contributor to HORIZON. *He is a long-time student of Roman influences on the Western world.*

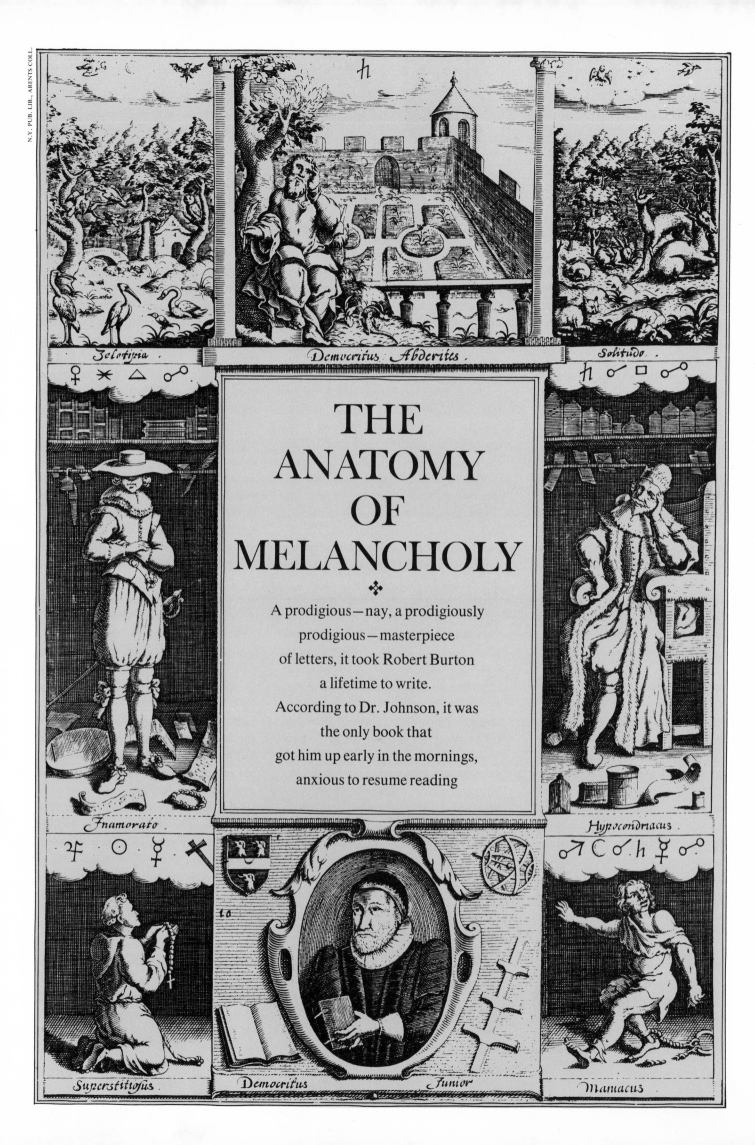

THE ANATOMY OF MELANCHOLY

A prodigious—nay, a prodigiously
prodigious—masterpiece
of letters, it took Robert Burton
a lifetime to write.
According to Dr. Johnson, it was
the only book that
got him up early in the mornings,
anxious to resume reading

E very age has its own peculiar disease of the spirit. Thus the medieval religious were attacked by that sloth of the soul called accidie, which often struck before lunchtime and hence was called the noonday devil. The fashionable intellectual ailment of Baudelaire's Paris was spleen—a sort of ill temper blown up into cosmic dissatisfaction. Our own age has known angst, or atomic anxiety, as well as *la noia* (Alberto Moravia's refinement of the French *ennui*). The great spiritual illness of the age of Shakespeare and Ben Jonson was melancholy.

The term literally means "black bile." The old mechanistic view of the psyche, accepting that matter was made up of earth, air, fire, and water, saw in the structure of man's soul an analogous fourfold mixing of elements. These were called humors, and they were, in fact, a collection of ultimate fluids—blood, phlegm, yellow bile, and black bile. In a healthy, balanced human personality there was no preponderance of one over the other. But an excess of blood produced a sanguine temperament; too much phlegm made a man phlegmatic; yellow bile in overplus caused choler, or the habit of anger. Exceed the normal secretion of black bile, and the gloom and depression of a melancholy fit resulted, or

A portion of the title page, with center panel removed (opposite), of the 1638 edition of The Anatomy of Melancholy *contains engravings showing several types of melancholic sufferers. The left-hand column includes, from the top, the jealous, symbolized by birds in a moonlit garden; the enamored, or lovesick, personified by a down-at-the-mouth dandy; the superstitious, by a friar telling his beads (Burton was a stout Protestant). The right-hand column includes, from the top, the solitary, symbolized by the more timid forms of wildlife; the hypochondriacal, personified by a bookish worrier; the maniacal, by a ragged lunatic in chains. Top center is Burton's intellectual hero, the Greek philosopher Democritus of Abdera. Bottom center is a portrait of the melancholy Burton, who went by the pen name Democritus Junior.*

else a chronic state of melancholy. All nonsense, of course, but we still use the terms: "I'm not exactly sanguine about the outcome of the conference"; "That raised my choler, I can tell you" —and so on. The general term "humor" has been simplified into merely good and bad, as in "The good humor man's in a pretty bad humor." "Humorous" means plain funny, but when Hamlet, just before the players arrive, talks about the "humorous man," he means an emotional actor, one sick with an excess of temperament (or humor). The hero of Fletcher's *Humorous Lieutenant* is brave because of a disordering of his humors; he's not a comic.

Humors were very much a property of the English theatre in the later days of Queen Elizabeth I and the early days of her successor, James. Playwrights like George Chapman and Ben Jonson revived the medieval doctrine of humors in order to create clear-cut satirical types for their comedies. It was with Chapman that the stock melancholic character first appeared—Dowsecer in *A Humorous Day's Mirth*, black-suited, black-hatted, to match his bile. The black hat (like Stephen Dedalus's in Joyce's *Ulysses*) became a recognizable attribute of the professional gloomy man, so that of a later playwright it was said:

Deep in a dump John Ford alone was got,
With folded arms and melancholy hat.

When Hamlet first walked onto the stage of The Globe, sad-faced and all in black, the audience probably expected a "humorous man." But Shakespeare's psychology was too subtle to settle for such mechanical simplifications as pleased Ben Jonson. Hamlet is Hamlet, and no medieval analyst could explain his sickness.

Melancholy was a stage cult, and it inevitably led to self-conscious postures of gloom and misery in real life. Real life likes to imitate art, especially if it has nothing better to do, and our own age has seen, chiefly among the young, imitation Bonnie and Clydes and Midnight Cowboys. The Elizabethan Inns

of Court were probably full of mock Dowsecers; long faces under black became the rage. But this Tudor-Stuart melancholy was more than a pose or a device of the theatre. After the swelling tide of Elizabethan expansion—the defeat of the Armada, pirated wealth flowing in, the chauvinism of a little country aware for the first time of its muscles—there came a large depression. There was a mixture of causes. The year of *Hamlet*, 1601, was a bad year because it saw the Essex rebellion and the execution of Essex, once England's chivalric flower. The queen was old; there was worry over the succession. When James I came to the throne, and the worry was ended, there was still a general sense that things were not as good as they used to be. Gloucester in *King Lear* sums it all up: "We have seen the best of our time: machinations, hollowness, treachery, and all ruinous disorders, follow us disquietly to our graves."

Well, the machinations and treachery were certainly there at court, and high office was rarely attained through merit. And all the time prices were rising. The settled economy of the Middle Ages had given way to a transitional system that was not clearly understood. As well as a shortage of money, there was a strong sense of the omnipresence of the Grim Reaper. Infant mortality was high, the plague struck and struck again, and there was none of the medieval acceptance of death as the gateway to a greater life. There was, then, plenty to be melancholy about.

Of course, there has always been plenty to be melancholy about, and there always will be. But the fact of melancholy, the very name (as telling as our thalidomide or lung cancer), was so rubbed into the intellectuals of the age that it seemed to be a *fin-de-siècle* monopoly. Even Sir John Harington's cleanly invention of the water closet was dragged into the house of intellectual gloom. A water closet was a good thing to sit upon and costively brood. Why the melancholy Jaques in

As You Like It? Because a jakes was a john, and John-Jaques's sardonic disquisitions suited best a prolonged session, preferably solitary, on the stool. Shakespeare saw that melancholy could be laughed at, not cruelly but with the salutary derision proper for self-indulgence. For melancholy could be enjoyed, and still can be.

When I go musing all alone,
Thinking of divers things foreknown
When I build castles in the air,
Void of sorrow and void of fear,
Pleasing myself with phantasms sweet,
Methinks the time runs very fleet.
    All my joys to this are folly,
    Naught so sweet as melancholy.

That doggerel, which anticipates the spirit if not the poetry of Milton's *Il Penseroso,* was written by the great philosopher of melancholy, Robert Burton. Melancholy to him was a term that could encompass many states of mind—mild regret, peaceful contemplation (which is all it seems to have meant to Milton), bitter grief, the hatching of pleasing visions, jealous torments, dementia:

I'll change my state with any wretch,
Thou canst from gaol or dunghill fetch;
My pain's past cure, another hell,
I may not in this torment dwell!
Now desperate I hate my life,
Lend me a halter or a knife;
    All my griefs to this are jolly,
    Naught so damn'd as melancholy.

These lines, and many, many more, come from the preliminaries to Burton's *Anatomy of Melancholy*—the greatest work ever written on the subject, and by far the longest. It is a leisurely book of half a million words, which has room not only for a verse preludium but for a preface—"Democritus Junior to the Reader"—as long as many a modern novel, as well as for the first study of climatology, "A Digression of the Air"; a pioneering examination of the psychology of sex; a multitude of good stories (which have inspired, among other works, the *Lamia* of Keats, Christopher Fry's *A Phoenix Too Frequent,* and my own *The Eve of St. Venus*); the first serious study of the morbid effects of too much religion; a compendium of classical literature (Byron told Thomas Moore that it was the most useful book in the world for "a man who wishes to acquire a reputation of being well read, with the least trouble"); and pleas for pacifism, better roads, canals, marsh reclamation, economic tariffs, and old-age pensions. But essentially it is, in Sir William Osler's words, "the greatest medical treatise written by a layman." It first appeared in 1621, two years before the first folio of Shakespeare's plays and five years after Shakespeare's death. It is one of the few books that one regrets Shakespeare was unable to read in his retirement.

As for Burton, his life was all retirement. Born in Leicestershire in 1577, fourth of a family of nine, he settled early to the life of a scholar and pluralist clergyman. He entered Brasenose College in 1593, was elected a student of Christ Church in 1599, and became a bachelor of divinity in 1614. Then he became vicar of St. Thomas's in Oxford and later got the living of Seagrave in his native county. He seems not to have had a powerful call to the ministry (the church was probably all that was open to a man of his bookish temperament), and we are possibly justified in seeing him as a not over-zealous incumbent, glad to leave the pulpit and get back to his library. This library, which he bequeathed in part to the Bodleian, had about two thousand volumes in it. Overwhelmed by the massive but lightly carried learning of the *Anatomy,* we see him as a man who lived for books, a giant of the shelves like Dr. Johnson. (Dr. Johnson, incidentally, said that the *Anatomy* was the only book that got him up early in the mornings, anxious to resume reading.)

On his own admission, Burton's life was uneventful. "I have lived," he said, "a silent, sedentary, solitary, private life, *mihi et musis* in the university, as long almost as Xenocrates in Athens, *ad senectam fere,* to learn wisdom as he did, penned up most part in my study."

One can imagine that Burton suffered from the concomitants of such slippered retirement—indigestion, sluggish liver, an unseemly sexual continence. Certainly he suffered from melancholy, and he confessed that he wrote his masterwork in order to cure it. But the only cure he seems to have found for his gloomy fits was, according to Bishop Kennett, to leave his study in Christ Church and walk down to Folly Bridge. There he would find bargees slanging each other, and their vigorous exchange of language gave him refreshment. There is no evidence that he himself was slanged and slanged back. Dr. Johnson, it will be remembered, answered an insolent waterman with "Sir, your wife, under the pretence of keeping a bawdy-house, is a receiver of stolen goods." But it seems that Burton was always a spectator and auditor of life, though he would talk wittily and volubly enough —"very merry, facete and juvenile" is Anthony Wood's description of his conversation—with other scholars.

There are three extant portraits of Burton—a painted bust in the cathedral at Oxford, an oil painting at Brasenose, and an engraved miniature, which forms part of the symbolic frontispiece of the *Anatomy.* The face is shy, thoughtful, intelligent, diffident, above all genial. He accepted his melancholy as part of the Adamic inheritance and made the best of things. That he was a humorist in our sense of the word we need no biographical facts to attest: *The Anatomy of Melancholy* is, by a magnificent and somehow very English irony, one of the great comic works of the world. Not comic by dogged intention, nor by the pathetic accident that makes what is meant to be grave (an illiterate epitaph, for instance) unconsciously funny. Burton's humor is, in fact, a natural fluid that washes everything he writes, a temperamental secretion that characterizes every sentence. Let us draw a deep breath and then take in one of Burton's saltier periods:

Love is blind, as the saying is, Cupid's blind, and so are all his followers. . . . Every lover admires his mistress, though she be very deformed of herself, ill-favoured, wrinkled, pimpled, pale, red, yellow, tanned, tallow-faced, have a swollen juggler's platter face, or a thin, lean, chitty face, have clouds in her face, be crooked, dry, bald, goggle-eyed, blear-eyed, or with staring eyes, she looks like a squis'd cat, hold her head still awry, heavy, dull, hollow-eyed, black or yellow about the eyes, or squint-eyed, sparrow-mouthed, Persian hook-nosed, have a sharp fox-nose, a red nose, China flat, great nose, *nare simo patuloque* [snub and flat nose], a nose like a promontory, gubber-tushed, rotten teeth, black, uneven, brown teeth, beetle-browed, a witch's beard, her breath stink all over the room, her nose drop winter and summer, with a Bavarian poke under her chin, a sharp chin, laveeared, with a long crane's neck, which stands awry too, *pendulis mammis,* "her dugs like two double jugs," or else no dugs, in that other extreme, bloody-fallen fingers, she have filthy, long unpared nails, scabbed hands or wrists, a tanned skin, a rotten carcass, crooked back, she stoops, is lame, splay-footed, "as slender in the middle as a cow in the waist," gouty legs, her ankles hang over her shoes, her feet stink, she breed lice, a mere changeling, a very monster, an oaf imperfect, her whole complexion savours, an harsh voice, incondite gesture, vile gait, a vast virago, or an ugly tit, a slug, a fat fustilugs, a truss, a long lean rawbone, a skeleton . . . and to thy judgment looks like a mard in a lanthorn, whom thou couldst not fancy for a world, but hatest, loathest, and wouldest have spit in her face, or blow thy nose in her bosom, *remedium amoris* to another man, a dowdy, a slut, a scold, a nasty, rank, rammy, filthy, beastly quean, dishonest peradventure, obscene, base, beggarly, rude, foolish, untaught, peevish, Irus' daughter . . . Grobian's scholar; if he love her once, he admires her for all this, he takes no notice of any such errors or imperfections of body or mind,

Ipsa hæc
Delectant, veluti Balbinum polypus Agnæ

[These are the very things that charm him, as Agna's polypus charmed Balbinus];

he had rather have her than any woman in the world.

This Rabelaisian effort is Burton all out, making up the sentence as he goes along and, like Shakespeare, not blotting a line. As he writes, apt quotations from the classics come to him unbid-

The four basic temperaments to which the body fluids, or humors, give rise are symbolized in a set of sixteenth-century engravings.

den, and down they go to swell the flood of words. His writing is like talk, learned but earthy, and once he starts he is hard to stop. We can hear the voice very clearly—clean, dry, a little tremulous, hardly stemmed by coughs, chuckles, occasional (I swear I can hear this) tooth-sucking, the odd ripe nose-blow, the voice of a man who evidently is not in the habit of talking to ladies.

That passage comes from the long

section on love melancholy, and to anyone who does not know Burton but would like to dip into him, this is the section I recommend to start on. It exhausts its subject and very nearly the reader. First he divides up love according to its object—animal, vegetable, mineral, abstract, artifact ("Things without life, made by art, pictures, sports, games, sensible objects, as hawks, hounds, horses"). He then gets down to what he nicely terms "Heroical or love-Melancholy," its power, its distribution throughout the animal world, the circumstances of its arousal ("Stars, temperature, full diet, place, country, clime, condition, idleness . . . Artificial allurements, and provocations of lust and love, gestures, apparel, dowry, money, etc."), and its symptoms ("Dryness, paleness, leanness, waking, sighing, etc." in the body, and in the mind "Fear, sorrow, suspicion, anxiety, etc. A hell, torment, fire, blindness, etc. Dotage, slavery, neglect of business."). Note that falling in love is assumed to be a one-sided matter: it is Romeo sighing for Rosaline, not in bed with Juliet. It is an ailment, an impairment of vision foretold in Shakespeare's *Midsummer Night's Dream,* where "The lunatic, the lover and the poet are of imagination all compact."

There are various cures for the disease—"labour, diet, physic, abstinence . . . good counsel, persuasion . . . philters, magical and poetical cures," and so on—but the best cure of all is what most of us would regard as the only possible one: "To let them have their desire." This is how, with characteristic coruscations of Latin, Burton puts it:

The last refuge and surest remedy, to be put into practice in the utmost place, when no other means will take effect, is to let them go together, and enjoy one another:

Potissima cura est ut heros amasia sua potiatur, saith Guianerius, *cap.* 15, *tract.* 15. Æsculapius himself, to this malady, cannot invent a better remedy, *quam ut amanti cedat amatum* (Jason Pratensis), than that a lover have his desire. . . . 'Tis the special cure, to let them bleed *in vena hymenœia,* for love is a pleurisy, and if it be possible, so let it be, *optataque gaudia carpant.* Arculanus holds it the speediest and the best cure, 'tis Savonarola's last precept, a principal infallible remedy, the last, sole, and safest refuge.

Julia, sola potes nostras extinguere flammas,
Non nive, non glacie, sed potes igne pari.

Julia alone can quench my desire,
With neither ice nor snow, but with like fire.

But before we reach this conclusion, which first has to be debated at great length, we wander through a kind of delectable nightmare of old tales and classical allusions, superstitions ancient and Jacobean. It is not enough to say that a man will risk all for love; the proposition has to be exhaustively illustrated: "And as Peter Abelhardus lost his testicles for his Helonissa, he will (I say) not venture an incision, but life itself. For how many gallants offered to lose their lives for a night's lodging with Cleopatra in those days!" And so on and so on and so on. The wood of argument is sturdily there, but we cannot see it for the trees of exemplification.

Burton is not a scientist by our standards, though his ostensible aim is to throw the sweet light of reason and order upon certain aspects of human behavior. He is rather a sort of rough-and-ready artist who impresses with the bludgeon of volubility instead of with the refining file of Horace or the painful scrupulosity of Henry James. "He is," said Holbrook Jackson once, "an artist in literary mosaic, using the shreds and patches he has torn from the work of others to make a picture emphatically his own." Traditionally, art makes use of the raw material provided by nature; Burton's material is artificial, man-made. His approach, if not his discursive technique, brings him close to the pop artists of our day, who make their pictures out of newspaper clippings and soup labels. But a chunk of Virgil or Macrobius is somewhat more enlightening than a shred torn from a comic strip or a Coke bottle-top. Burton contains the whole of the classical world; he makes a massive puppet show out of the great figures that, for most of us, must lie dead in the dust. Montaltus, Fuchsius, Laurentius, Hildesheim, Maginus, Scaliger, Mantuan, Gasper Vilela, Sallust, Balthasar Castilio, Galateus, Camerarius, Nicephorus, and Sir Henry Spelman are reanimated so that their wisdom may caper briefly before us. But there is only one master, the one with the strings.

Burton's approach to his work was cumulative, additive, like that of Joyce creating *Finnegans Wake.* The first edition of the *Anatomy,* published when he was a fresh and vigorous forty-four, was a fat enough quarto—nine hundred pages. The four editions that followed in the next seventeen years saw it swell lustily, outgrowing the quarto format and demanding the grown-up suit of a small folio. After Burton's death in 1640, without the sharpness of that overseeing eye and the delight in fresh embroidery, the book became a set property for the printers to do with as they liked, and the final edition of the century—the graceless folio of 1676—is a thin-papered mess of typographical errors attesting the fact that an age with no relish for melancholy had begun. It was not until 1799, the age of the melancholy romantics, the Gothick men, and such loving antiquaries as Charles Lamb, that the *Anatomy* came back into its own. But Lamb was unhappy about the reprint. "What need was there," he said, "of unearthing the bones of that fantastic old great man, to expose them in a winding-sheet of the newest fashion to modern censure? What hapless stationer could dream of Burton becoming popular?" Yet if remaining in print is a test of popularity, then Burton has remained quietly popular for the last century and a half. At this moment, though, his reputation seems to have suffered a certain depression. When I took the theme of a novella out of the *Anatomy,* there were certain critics who turned up their noses and murmured: "Good God! He's old stuff, the sort of otiose bookworm most likely to be turned out of the Electronic Village; life is too short to settle down with a highball and Burton."

All I can say is that most modern books weary me, but Burton never does. I'm always learning new things from him, or things so old as to have become new again. I can still find no better recipe than this as a cure for depression:

Exercise not too remiss, nor too violent. Sleep a little more than ordinary. Excrements daily to be voided by art or nature; and, which Fernelius enjoins his patient, *consil.* 44, above the rest, to avoid all passions and perturbations of the mind. Let him not be alone or idle (in any kind of melancholy), but still accompanied with such friends and familiars he most affects, neatly dressed, washed, and combed, according to his ability at least, in clean sweet linen, spruce, handsome, decent, and good apparel; for nothing sooner dejects a man than want, squalor, and nastiness, foul or old clothes out of fashion.

Might not some of the disaffected young know an accession of comparative calm and happiness if they followed a prescription like that? And here, in the face of the prohibitionists, is ample authority for an occasional period of intoxication. Wine is the drink, though, not spirits:

"No better physic" (saith Rhasis) "for a melancholy man: and he that can keep company, and carouse, needs no other medicines," 'tis enough. His countryman Avicenna, 31 *Doct.* 2, *cap.* 8, proceeds farther yet, and will have him that is troubled in mind, or melancholy, not to drink only, but now and then to be drunk: excellent good physic it is for this and many other diseases. Magninus, *Reg. san. part.* 3, *cap.* 31, will have them to be so once a month at least, and gives his reasons for it, "because it scours the body by vomit, urine, sweat, of all manner of superfluities, and keeps it clean."

And with our wine we may smoke "Tobacco, divine, rare, superexcellent tobacco, which goes far beyond all the panaceas, potable gold, and philosophers' stones, a sovereign remedy to all diseases."

If our epoch considers that there is more to existence than what Edmund Burke called "living pleasant" and not taxing ourselves with world sorrow, then we shall find in Burton enough strong intellectual meat to sustain our meditations on war, government, racism, education, law, public morals. He has a good hit, for instance, at the American philanthropists who make their endowments in no very sincere spirit, calling their Jacobean equivalents

gouty benefactors who, when by fraud or rapine they have extorted all their lives, oppressed whole provinces, societies, etc., give something to pious uses, build a satisfactory almshouse, school or bridge, etc., at their last end, or before perhaps, which is no otherwise than to steal a goose and stick down a feather, rob a thousand to relieve ten.

And here is a comment on war:

. . . so many bloody battles, so many thousands slain at once, such streams of blood able to turn mills [through one person's mad guilt] whilst statesmen themselves in the meantime are secure at home, pampered with all delights and pleasures, take their ease and follow their lusts, not considering what intolerable misery poor soldiers endure, their often wounds, hunger, thirst, etc.; the lamentable cares, torments, calamities, and oppressions that accompany such proceedings, they feel not, take no notice of it.

Sometimes, unfortunately, Burton seeks reform of the world through some dictatorial character:

We had need of some general visitor in our age that . . . might root out barbarism in America . . . cure us of our epidemical

diseases . . . end all our idle controversies, cut off our tumultuous desires, inordinate lusts; root out atheism, impiety, heresy, schism, and superstition, which now so crucify the world, catechize gross ignorance; purge Italy of luxury and riot, Spain of superstition and jealousy, Germany of drunkenness, all our northern countries of gluttony and intemperance; castigate our hard-hearted parents, masters, tutors; lash disobedient children, negligent servants; correct these spendthrifts and prodigal sons, enforce idle persons to work, drive

CHRIST CHURCH, OXFORD

The inscription on Burton's tomb, at Oxford, attests his lifelong dedication to his humor.

drunkards off the alehouse, repress thieves, visit corrupt and tyrannizing magistrates, etc.

That is a Presidential program suitable for Sinclair Lewis's Buzz Windrip.

Burton sees bad in the world, as we all do, but he does not expect things to get any better. We are born to original sin, and all our woes stem from Adam's fall. There is no health in us:

How many diseases there are, is a question not yet determined; Pliny reckons up 300 from the crown of the head to the sole of the foot: elsewhere he saith, *morborum*

infinita multitudo, their number is infinite. Howsoever it was in those times, it boots not; in our days I am sure the number is much augmented . . . For besides many epidemical diseases unheard of, and altogether unknown to Galen and Hippocrates, as *scorbutum,* smallpox, *plica,* sweating sickness, *morbus Gallicus,* etc., we have many proper and peculiar almost to every part.

He would not be surprised to hear how the number has been augmented since his time—polio, pulmonary carcinoma, athlete's foot, and the rest. But Burton's strength, and the ultimate cause of his cheerfulness, lies in an incapacity for disappointment: he already knows the worst. All that remains to be done is to attempt cures where cures are possible, and where there is no cure, to seek what palliatives art and nature provide. Let us relieve the fundamental melancholy that is woven into the human fabric by partaking of the infinite solace of the world—wine, venery, the bad language of bargees, talk, taletelling, and most of all, books. It is in the curious wisdom of old writers that we find the materials for the only utopia that will ever be realized—a utopia of the imagination. To despair is stupid, to think sublunary bliss is possible is even more stupid. Burton ends his huge book with very simple maxims:

Only take this for a corollary and conclusion, as thou tenderest thine own welfare in this and all other melancholy, thy good health of body and mind, observe this short precept, give not way to solitariness and idleness. "Be not solitary, be not idle."

Latin has the last word, as in Burton it must: *"Sperate miseri, cavete felices"*— "If you are unhappy, hope; if you are happy, beware." It is a good, cautious counsel to carry through an imperfect world.

Anthony Burgess is a prolific critic and novelist. One of his novels, A Clockwork Orange, *a vision of a future in which gangs of young hoodlums terrorize the world, is being made into a motion picture directed by Stanley Kubrick.*

THE DUTY OF THE PRINCE IS MAGNIFICENCE

The four sons of King John took up their noble burdens with a tasteful zeal. They collected pearls and tapestries, illuminated books and lapis lazuli, ermine and statues, and tennis courts and rubies. When they died, exhausted by one of history's most extravagant spending sprees, they left behind collections that were in themselves works of art

By MORRIS BISHOP

When times are prosperous, the artist thrives, living high and heedless. When dark depressions come, he is the first to suffer, while the collector has his day. The collector no doubt desires to forget the encompassing woe in the contemplation of beauty; but he buys cheap, hoards, gloats. His urge is to possess, to secure, to survive the evil days with his collection augmented.

The latter years of the fourteenth century and the early years of the fifteenth were the grimmest period in French history. The Black Death of 1348 and the lesser plagues that followed destroyed at least a third of France's people. The everlasting war with England, a four-hundred-year war with long truces, erupted into bloody activity. Plundering raids, official and private, crisscrossed French territory. Taxes and forced levies robbed the poor of their few possessions. The voice of the people was a long cry of pain.

While France agonized, the rich collected. The example was set by King John II and his sons.

King John succeeded to the French throne in 1350. He was commonly called, and still is, Jean le Bon; but "le Bon" could be pronounced with a mocking intonation, to suggest that a better epithet would be "the Stupid." One modern historian calls him "that knightly muddle-head," and another "that brainless paladin"; a third rates him "among the worst of medieval French kings." He was slow-witted, obstinate, greedy, and capricious in the beheading of his advisers. But he loved pretty things, jewels, goldsmithery, materials, furniture. In fourteen years of tragedy and turmoil he managed to buy 235 tapestries. He patronized artists, craftsmen, and men of letters, who naturally termed him "the Good" without irony.

King John had four sons: Charles, the dauphin, destined for the throne; Louis, Duke of Anjou; John, who was to become Duke of Berry; and Philip, the future Duke of Burgundy.

The nearly permanent war with the English came to a climax in 1356. Edward, the Black Prince, commanded the English. Outnumbered, he took up a strong defensive position near Poitiers. King John and his sons led the French in a gallant but foolish attack. In the hot action King John wielded a mighty battle-axe, but it was a time for generalship, not knightly prowess. When fortune frowned, he ordered his four sons to the rear. The elder sons obeyed, some said all too readily; but fourteen-year-old Philip joined his father, warding off attackers. When the two were captured, Philip heard an Englishman sneer at his father; though the boy was wounded, he smote the offender in the face. At Poitiers Philip gained the sobriquet "le Hardi," the Bold, which he bore proudly for the rest of his life. But the battle was lost, and John and Philip were carried off to England.

The royal visitors were royally received. There is a cousinly solidarity among princes, as strong as nationalism, or stronger. The visitors were lodged in comfortable castles (at Windsor for a time) and were entertained with hunts, tourneys, and cock-

fights. Dainties were imported for their table, and wines from Languedoc (the king sold off his surplus; buyers reported it to be sour). The prisoners were served by a staff of seventy-one Frenchmen, including an astrologer, a jester, and a "king of minstrels." King John sent for his court painter, Girard d'Orléans, and paid him the handsome salary of six shillings a day. It was perhaps in England that Girard painted the famous representation of his master, which is one of the first French panel portraits known and may be the first realistic portrait of modern times.

Young Philip enforced his reputation for truculence. In a quarrel over chess he drew his sword to attack the Black Prince. While a guest at the English king's table he sprang up to prevent the maître d'hôtel from serving the king of England before the king of France. Edward III took this protest as a joke: "God knows, cousin, you have merited your nickname of the Bold."

France, for some reason, longed to have her monarch back. After four years the terms were settled. Of these, the most onerous was the payment of a gigantic ransom of three million gold crowns. The king was released so that he might raise the ransom, while three of his sons and a band of high nobles submitted to captivity as hostages for him. The king used every device to collect his ransom money, grinding most of it out of the wretched poor. In the end he was a million crowns short. Then his son Louis d'Anjou broke his parole and returned to France. King John was shocked and humiliated by such conduct. He returned voluntarily to London, being a proper gentleman and either the Good or the Stupid. He was warmly greeted by his English friends and was pleasantly quartered in the Hôtel de Savoie, the hospitable traditions of which are carried on at the same site by the Savoy Hotel. He then solved a good many problems by dying, in April, 1364.

John the Good was succeeded by his son Charles V, "le Sage"—the Wise, or perhaps better, the Sensible. Froissart calls him *"durement sages et soutils"*—harshly wise and cunning. He was delicate, suffering from poor circulation, neuralgia, perhaps ulcers. More diplomat than soldier, he enjoyed calm and peace, church services, and conversation. He had thought of entering the priesthood, and was phenomenally chaste, forbidding men's short jackets and women's tight dresses on moral grounds. He took his pleasure listening to music and to readings from the Bible and instructive histories. He was curious about science, especially astrology and medicine, and sometimes invited professors from the university for an evening of serious talk. He was regarded as a philosopher by the vulgar, not by the philosophers.

Charles accepted withal the principle of "magnificence" as the duty of the prince. Even in those hardest of hard times the king, emblem and embodiment of his kingdom, was expected to represent its pride through display and generosity. The cheering crowds, mystically bound to their master, felt an emotional sharing in his public splendor and rejoiced in his

A gathering of royal art patrons includes, standing from left, the dukes of Burgundy, Berry, and Anjou. Seated is their brother, Charles V. Immediately to the left of the king is the aged Philip of Orléans, uncle of the four brothers. At far right is the Dauphin, who became Charles VI in 1380 and went mad in 1392. The miniature is from a 1410 French manuscript of Saint Augustine's City of God.

processions and festivals, though they themselves were due to pay the scot. Pomp and circumstance filled the commoners with religious awe. Charles built fine castles, including the Bastille and a pleasure palace near Paris, sweetly named Beauté. He transformed and embellished Vincennes and the Louvre with sculptures, stained-glass windows, wainscotings, tapestries (he had more than two hundred). And he collected. At his Melun castle alone he possessed twenty-seven crucifixes of gold and twenty-seven of silver, seventy-two silver statuettes, sixty-three altar dressings, forty-seven royal crowns, seven dozen gold plates, and six dozen gold spoons. Most splendid were his twenty-six nefs (properly ships), imposing structures set on the lord's dining table, containing his cup, spoon, fork, a deposit of spices, and a "touchpiece" to detect poisons. Some nefs represented castles; others were adorned with human figures, lions, dolphins, eagles, or angels. To the nef every guest and servant bowed, as to a shrine. Among the other items in Charles's inventory were silver bells and whistles, toys, mirrors, checkerboards, and cups made of ostrich eggs set in silver.

Charles's library, of about a thousand manuscript volumes, was the source of the present Bibliothèque Nationale. It was rich in French romances and in religion, philosophy, law, and science, including sixty works on medicine and surgery. The books were evidently chosen rather for their con-

tent than for their physical qualities. The library was established in richly decorated rooms in a tower of the Louvre, with gratings on the windows "to keep out birds and other animals." Could these have been insect screens? Flies and midges are a worse menace to scribes and illuminators than birds and beasts are.

The artists who produced the court's elegances were treated as respectable craftsmen. Painters were members of the saddlers' guild; sculptors were stonecutters. Some, however, as *varlets de chambre,* had access to the king's person and friendship. They were expected to turn their hands to anything, the decoration of furniture and court carriages, the painting of innumerable pennons and banners for the army. (When Girard d'Orléans was in England with John the Good, he made a chess set for his master.) The artists illuminated manuscripts and painted altarpieces with representations of the donors. The time of secular panel-painting was barely beginning. Had such works of art existed, there would have been no place to display them; or perhaps it is better to say that because there was no place to display them they did not exist. One cannot hang pictures on the stone walls of castle interiors.

Charles V died of accumulated ills in 1380, leaving the throne to his twelve-year-old son, Charles VI, a flighty and unpromising youth. The dying king named to the regency his three brothers, Louis d'Anjou, Jean de Berry, and Philippe de Bourgogne. His eyes had hardly closed when the eldest brother, Louis d'Anjou, seized his jewels and treasures, reckoned to be worth nineteen million francs, and tried to impose himself as sole regent. Defeated by the younger brothers, he undertook to enforce his claims to the kingdom of Naples, and while on a disastrous campaign he died there of disease in 1384.

Louis d'Anjou shared the family delight in magnificence, but his taste is said to have been more ostentatious than discriminating. The incomplete inventory of his possessions lists 3,600 items, mostly jewels, goldsmiths' work, and tapestries. Even his battle dress was richly jeweled and gold-inlaid. His helmet was adorned with gold, pearls, and diamonds and was surmounted by a gold fleur-de-lis. The learned historian Joan Evans describes his nef representing the Fountain of Youth, with fifty-four figures in the round, "some coming in litters or walking on crutches or riding on mules to the magical fountain, some making ready and casting off their shoes, and others bathing in its waters. The body of the vessel was decorated with people crying their wares as they might in the streets of Paris, and with dances of men and women."

Even the pot stand for his kitchen was fabricated of silver, "decorated at the top with a seated figure of the chef in a long gown and a high cap, holding a sausage. Beneath him stood a figure of the turnspit in a short coat holding a spit with a goose upon it; a cook's boy with two partridges, and, on the other side, the porter carrying in the carcass of a sheep and an under-cook with a roast sucking-pig." This is a good example of the realism that was characteristic of fourteenth-century French art.

With Louis d'Anjou out of the way, his two brothers ruled France until Charles VI assumed control at the age of twenty. Four years later, in 1392, the young king went suddenly insane, attacking his familiars with his sword. In his recurring fits he was convinced that he was made of glass; sometimes he barked like a dog or ran howling like a werewolf. His queen abandoned him out of fear; loose women were brought into the palace to substitute for her. For thirty years the king suffered prolonged and increasing attacks of madness, while the enemies of France brought her lower and lower. Meanwhile, the two uncles regained rule as regents for the mad monarch, adding to their power and wealth and noteworthily to their collections.

The elder uncle, Jean, Duc de Berry, was more intellectual than warrior, more a puller of strings than a wielder of battle-axes. Christine de Pisan, one of the first professional women writers, describes him as handsome, amiable, wise in counsel, cautious in action, "of sweet and kindly intercourse with no prideful hauteur, benignant in address and response, cheery in conversation, and in all things very considerate." But Christine, who lived by the favor of great patrons, could remark no evil in them. Others reported Duke John to be debauched, spendthrift, and little esteemed in the kingdom. Certainly he outdid all his predecessors in the harshness of his tax collections. The people toiled and suffered to support art. This, he thought, was a good thing. Maybe it was, if art is greater than life.

At any rate, Duke John was a great builder, art patron, and collector. He built seventeen important castles and other edifices, most of them now in ruins or in dust. He restored the castle of Poitiers, with its superb great hall, and supplied the central façade of the cathedral at Bourges. He had his own staff of jewelers and goldsmiths, and his own artists, some of whom, like Jacquemart de Hesdin and the Limbourg brothers, are by no means forgotten. He appointed the painter André Beauneveu his commissioner for the arts; he also had a purchasing agent in Italy, one of the first art dealers. Duke John, wearing his hat adorned with sapphires, emeralds, rubies, and pearls, was himself an art object, a dazzlement, a chef-d'oeuvre in his own collection.

Duke John possessed a mountain of gems—diamonds, rubies, pearls, agates, jaspers, garnets, amethysts, rock crystals, cat's-eyes, toadstones, corals, more than fifteen hundred cameos and intaglios. He liked to break down crude bijouterie and have the stones reassembled according to his own designs.

Thus he made suitable reliquaries for a piece of Saint Lawrence's grill, a twig from the Burning Bush, the leg of a Holy Innocent, the head of one of the Eleven Thousand Virgins. He made shrines for the Virgin's wedding ring, for a wine cup used in the Marriage at Cana, for a scrap from the mantle of Elijah.

(One wonders at the profusion of jewels in the Middle Ages. Most of them came from India and the Orient; they were imported into the West in Roman days or by daring merchants in medieval times. Remember Marco Polo, who returned from the East with a fortune sewed uncomfortably into his clothes. The quantity of jewels in circulation steadily increased. Gems may be hidden or stolen; they are seldom lost. Their value, the product of beauty and rarity, is intrinsic; before the time of banks they represented the chief liquid assets of a prince or noble. And they constituted the most compact means of transferring wealth or of carrying travel funds, as refugees from warring countries in our time have found again.)

In Italy Duke John's agent bought Greek vases, sculptures, medals of Augustus and Tiberius, ancient coins. (Some of the coins he had to melt down and mint again to pay his troops during a long-lasting siege.) In his passion for collecting he would collect almost anything: tapestries from Arras, embroideries from Florence and England, leather hangings from Spain, a *Wunderkammer* of natural curiosities—a snake's jaws, a porcupine's quill, a giant's tooth (in fact, an elephant's molar). He even collected dogs; he is said to have possessed fifteen hundred, mostly, no doubt, in hunting packs at his country castles. But the banquet scene in his *Très Riches Heures* shows a dog on the floor and two puppies on the very table.

His chief passion was for books, which in his day were, of course, in manuscript. His library numbered about three hundred volumes, fewer than his brother Charles had owned, but chosen with more discrimination. Duke John loved the beauty and personality of books; he loved also to read their words. He was especially fond of romances of chivalry. At one time he ordered some low-standing ivory candlesticks "to hold candles for reading romances." A real bibliophile, he carried a precious Book of Hours to war with him. Confronting in the field of battle the English commander, the Duke of Bedford, another connoisseur, he arranged to postpone the engagement while Bedford visited him in his tent to inspect the treasure.

Under the patronage of Jean de Berry the art of book illustration found a new development. (We call the art usually by its medieval name, "illumination," but it surpassed the present sense of that word.) The decoration of books was originally an ecclesiastical art, practiced by monks for the glory of God. Their themes were devotional and traditional except for drawings to elucidate medical, botanical, or legal texts. By the thirteenth century book illustration and ornamentation became in some part a secular trade, in the hands of professionals in Paris and Italy.

In the early fourteenth century new concepts, purposes, and freedoms entered the world of art. The Sienese painters developed theories of perspective, modeling, and the treatment of light and shadow—three-dimensional art, in fact. About 1320 Jean Pucelle in Paris introduced coherent perspective and modeling by light and shade. His successors set their figures in the round against a receding landscape, with close observation and rendering of detail. Such techniques promoted the concept of realism, or naturalism, that is, the exact rendering of reality. The concept was foreshadowed in the work of observant artists in England, Picardy, and the Netherlands; it took form in Italian wall-painting and migrated to French book-illustration; it then found its great efflorescence in the panel painting, or easel painting, of the Van Eycks and others in the Netherlands.

The style of painting that is known as the International Style became perceptible toward the end of the fourteenth century. The celebrated critic and scholar Erwin Panofsky pins down dates for the clear and conscious initiation of northern realism—1390 to 1395, the years when Jacquemart de Hesdin executed for Jean de Berry the *Très Belles Heures de Jehan de France, Duc de Berry,* which is now part of the "Brussels Hours." Panofsky says: "It is in the narrative miniatures of the 'Brussels Hours' that we witness the very beginning of naturalism in Northern landscape painting. . . . We have reached a new phase in the assimilation of the Trecento style, and, in a sense, a turning point in the history of Northern European painting."

At the same time, technical advances were made in the preparation of vellum and fine paper and in the composition and use of colors. The trade secrets were very precious. The historian Cartellieri notes that "a collaborator of Jacquemart de Hesdin, Jan van Holland, guarded the secrets of his colours so closely that once, when he suspected an assistant of having broken open his box, a fight with daggers ensued, and an artisan was left dead on the spot."

Jean de Berry, delighting in the new realism, gave its practitioners encouragement and employment. He commissioned, most notably, those Books of Hours that are today among the rarest and most precious treasures in the world's treasury of art.

The Book of Hours was a fourteenth-century innovation. It was a prayer book, a companion for the pious during church services, an aid to private devotions. The text was variable, suiting the convenience of the scribe. If one's attention wandered during the office, one could look at the pictures, which might stray far from the requirements of piety. The Book of Hours was a showpiece; as Panofsky says, it was part of a great lady's equipment, with her rosary, jewel box, and bottle of exotic scent.

The subjects of the illustrations were originally, and generally, pietistic. They were often arranged in the form of a "calendar," a series of pictures depicting the Christian year or the outward look of the successive months by their characteristic activities. In the hurly-burly of such activities the devotional purpose was likely to disappear. Early in the fourteenth century Jean Pucelle eliminated the figures, substituting the changing aspects of nature. This, says Panofsky, was a "revolutionary shift of interest."

The great masters of the Books of Hours were three brothers, Pol, John, and Herman, from Limbourg, in the Netherlands. After serving an apprenticeship in Paris they entered the employ of the Duc de Berry. Their masterpiece is the *Très Riches Heures,* now in Chantilly. It includes a calendar of the months; each picture shows a typical activity in the foreground, with a famous castle rising superbly, fantastically, in the background. The colors, especially the precious lapis lazuli, are pure and bright; the figures are rendered in the round, arrested in motion. Men and horses standing in sunlight cast shadows on the ground. This, we are told, is an "epochal innovation." The realism in detail is governed by a poetic, magical imagination, a suggestion of wonder, an escape from reality. Would it be indecent to mention here an illustrator-artist of modern times who sought and often captured the same spirit with a similar technique—Maxfield Parrish?

Perhaps there is another, almost secret quality in the *Très Riches Heures.* The acute Panofsky remarks that in the scenes of daily life there is a sharp distinction between the nobles and the poor: "the farmers and shepherds now suffer all the cold and do all the work whereas the Court of the Duc de Berry does all the feasting, hunting and love-making." But after all, this is a mere matter of common observation, hardly implying protest. If any social criticism was intended, it was surely imperceptible to the duke and his court. The most we dare say is that the contrast between rich and poor, between penury and magnificence, increases with deepening misery. The deprivations of the poor seem to provoke the ostentations of the rich.

Jean, Duc de Berry, outlived all his brothers and died in 1416. In his last moments his confessor enjoined him to return to the Abbey of St. Denis the great manuscript of the *Chroniques de France* that he had "borrowed." He was a collector to the last.

Philip the Bold, youngest of the four brothers and his father's favorite, was robust, but dark-complexioned and certainly not handsome. He had marked features and a jutting chin, which persisted among his distant descendants as the Hapsburg jaw. He was shrewd and long-sighted, affable and charming, and very much the *grand seigneur.* He enjoyed sports and hunting, dice playing and tennis; he lost enormous sums of money at the latter game. He was also extremely fastidious; he bathed in essence of violets or of damask roses.

His father had named him Duke of Burgundy, a semi-independent principality on the eastern edge of France with its capital in Dijon. Feudal wars and prudent marriages had added to it scattered territories within the empire. In 1369 he married Margaret of Flanders, the richest heiress in Europe, who brought to him the prosperous industrial region extending to the mouths of the Rhine on the North Sea. Hence his realm was part French, part Germanic, although its interests made it cleave rather to England and Germany than to France.

Philip's bride was purse-proud, imperious, and ill-humored, as well as ill-looking. But Philip was always devoted to her; there is no report of those supplemental loves so readily forgiven a monarch. He celebrated his marriage with such sumptuousness that four days afterward he was forced to pawn his last jewels. But he soon re-established his financial position. As a dominant member of the council of regency during the minority and lunacies of Charles VI he diverted enormous revenues to his own use.

He loved magnificence. For every event of importance he wore a completely new costume. At the coronation of Charles VI's queen, in 1389, he donned a velvet doublet decorated with forty sheep wearing bells of pearls at their necks and forty swans with pearls in their beaks. On a mission to the Duke of Lancaster he dazzled the assembly with his long-skirted tunic of black velvet embroidered with a rose branch bearing twenty-two begemmed roses. He changed into another adorned with sapphires and rubies surrounded with rosebuds of pearls (the rose theme complemented the emblem of Lancaster). He had a third costume of crimson velvet embroidered with a silver bear, its muzzle, collar, and leash composed of rubies and sapphires. He liked to wear cloth of gold (which must be very scratchy), elaborately jeweled hats, and ruby bracelets. He had a portable clock, which hung, like a camera, from a black silk ribbon about his neck. In one six-month period he and his son wore 217 pairs of gloves. He collected the skins of 9,408 ermines to line a dozen tunics and mantles. His duchess reflected his glorious sparkle. Her inventory lists 5 fine jeweled gold crowns, 30 necklaces, some 150 gold clasps, and gold belts studded with pearls, together with rings, garters, etc., etc.

Philip's insistence on magnificence sometimes defeated his more practical purposes. The French planned an invasion of England in 1386. The nobles vied with one another in decorating their ships. Philip, naturally, outdid them all. His flagship was painted gold and blue and bore nine great banners. The sails were stitched with his device, *Il me tarde* ("I can't wait"), surrounded by daisies in honor of his wife Margaret. His expeditionary force was supplied with three thousand banners proclaiming "I can't wait." But the decorations and other arrangements took so long that winter came and the invasion was called off.

Ten years later Philip helped organize a crusade against the Turks, who were advancing in what is now Bulgaria. He equipped his son and his army with dazzling armor and cos-

King John the Good, father of Charles V, is shown, in the fourteenth-century Chronicles *of Froissart, being captured by the English at Poitiers in 1356. The sumptuous castle of Poitiers was destroyed at that time, but rebuilt in the 1370's by John's son, the Duc de Berry.*

tumes, harnesses mounted with silver and gold, and twenty-four cartloads of green satin tents. But military competence was scanted, and the crusade ended in the disaster of Nicopolis, where the flower of Western chivalry was massacred by the Turks.

Magnificence wins no wars; it should stay at home. Philip adorned his realm with splendid structures and had them beautified by the greatest artists of his time. One of these at least, the sculptor Claus Sluter of Haarlem, deserves to be called a genius.

Conscious of mortality, Philip erected in Dijon a chartreuse, or charterhouse, for twenty-four Carthusian monks, whose duty was to pray unceasingly, day and night, for his soul (the great carry their privileges even into the next world). Claus Sluter supervised the work and began the sculptures, with the aid of his able assistant Claus de Werve. Only the portal, the winding stair, and the extraordinary Well of Moses remain. About the well stand six prophets, semi-detached from the structure, seeming to pose before it. They are vivid human portraits, executed with a realism still novel in their time. The prophet Jeremiah was originally equipped with a pair of copper spectacles. Jeremiah was, of course, commanded to write the words of the Lord in a book, but perhaps Sluter was making a glancing reference to his master, Philip, who was constantly withdrawing his gold-rimmed spectacles from their silver case.

The other great extant masterpiece of Claus Sluter is the tomb of Philip, begun long before his death. It stands now in the Dijon Museum. It is a pompous, full-length recumbent figure resting on a slab of black marble, surrounded by forty figures, thirty of them *pleurants,* or professional graveside lamenters, dressed in the conventional gowns of mutes. The figures are evidently not portraits but types, of courtiers, commoners, and monks. In expression and attitude, in the very droop of their robes, they communicate their grief to the observer.

In addition to sculptures, tapestries were Philip's particular delight. In the Middle Ages frescoes, though common in churches, were rare in castles, where the walls were rough, smoke-begrimed, and likely to exude damp. The rich preferred hangings, which gave some illusion of warmth and could be painted, embroidered, or woven to represent historical scenes or passages from the romances. The rich changed their tapestries with the seasons, or out of mere boredom. It was the fashion to use a tapestry as the background for the total décor of a room. King John the Good had an Easter set consisting of six green wall-tapestries with the arms of France in the corners, bed curtains and counterpane and bedside mat of green silk lined with blue linen, green serge window curtains, and chair cushions of blue and green silk.

In the fourteenth and fifteenth centuries came a boom in the tapestry business, centered in Paris and in Arras, which lay within the dominions of the dukes of Burgundy. Philip the Bold had an enormous collection of tapestries based on designs and cartoons by the leading artists. Some of them represented glorious episodes in his own career. A tapestry was his preferred gift to show favor to a courtier or foreign dignitary. There may have been a commercial factor in his lavishness. He obtained his tapestries cheap or for nothing from his factories; at small cost he advertised the art and industry of his weavers throughout the noble world.

Philip's library did not match those of his brothers Charles and John. His barber doubled as librarian; this is perhaps significant. About two hundred volumes are reported, including some fine illustrated books. But the collection is miscellaneous, a haphazard gathering. It reveals little of the owner's taste.

That taste is better indicated by descriptions of his country retreats. These were provided with summer arbors, tennis courts, salons, and baths. They were equipped also with surprises—a weather-conditioned room producing artificial rain, snow, and thunder, a concealed trap door dropping a heedless guest onto a bed of feathers, an ingenious water squirt designed to "wet the ladies under their petticoats." He also had a menagerie, including a bear, a porcupine, and a leopard so tame that children could ride on its back.

Philip died in April, 1404, in his sixty-third year. According to his wish, he was buried in a Carthusian robe borrowed from a humble monk. No doubt he hoped to influence, or even confuse, the Almighty Judge. But his funeral could hardly have escaped divine notice. It was a pageant, with two thousand nobles, bishops, monks, down to cooks and menials, all robed in mourning mantles. Thus they appear in Sluter's sculptures for Philip's tomb. The ceremonies were suitably magnificent and suitably extravagant. In order to pay for them, his heirs found it necessary to pawn his gold and silver tableware.

Where are they now, all the great collections, all the beautiful illuminated manuscripts and pictures, the gem-studded constructions of the goldsmiths?

The books have fared best. Many of Charles V's treasures descended to the Paris Bibliothèque Royale, which became our Bibliothèque Nationale. Almost a fourth of the manuscripts in Jean de Berry's inventory are to be found in the great European libraries. Philip the Bold's collection was kept intact at his death; most of it is now in the Bibliothèque des Ducs de Bourgogne, absorbed by the Brussels Bibliothèque Royale de Belgique. But many of the greatest books came, by one chance or another, into private hands. The *Très Riches Heures* was the pride of the princely Condé family; it now reposes in their château at Chantilly, which has gone public as the Musée Condé. Jean de Berry's *Apocalypse,* with no doubt other relics of the noble duke, is in the Pierpont Morgan Library.

The rich artifacts of gold and gems recorded in the inventories are harder to recognize and to trace. Many were given away to churches as spiritual tax-deductions or to diplomats as *douceurs.* Many were sold by royal heirs in periods of distress. Occasionally a monarch in need of cash picked the jewels from some glittering bauble and melted down the gold and silver. Proud castles were pillaged during the wars of religion and the Revolution. Fire took its toll, as in the burning of the Tuileries in 1871. Nevertheless some identifiable objects remain, such as a magnificent cup of Jean de Berry's in the British Museum.

And still the noble collectors remain, in history's long memory and, humbly, on typewritten cards in museum showcases. They take second billing, though, below the creators whom they patronized. The collectors deserve our recognition and gratitude, for a collection is itself a work of art. The passionate collector merges with his collection; he is himself a creator.

I give you a toast: to the Collector, to the ally of Beauty against Time.

Morris Bishop collects extravagant characters whose lives he often chronicles for HORIZON. *In the summer issue he wrote on "Father Boetti (or Sheik Mansour)." He is the author of the* HORIZON BOOK OF THE MIDDLE AGES, *published two years ago.*

CHARLES V, KING OF FRANCE

The anointing of Charles V in 1364 by the Archbishop of Rheims is depicted in one of Charles's many illuminated books. In the new art that he patronized, the King himself became a subject for artists.

HIS ROYAL LIBRARY

Like his younger ducal brothers, Charles V gathered into his possession every kind of art object there was to collect, from carved gems to castles. He was, however, a bibliophile above all else, and this is a fact of considerable significance in the evolution, or rather dissolution, of medieval culture. Until Charles's time the only serious repositories of learning were the monasteries. A man of learning himself, Charles seems to have been one of the first men to accumulate a library expressly for the use of his counselors. His library of twelve hundred manuscripts, including French translations that he himself had commissioned, became, fittingly, the nucleus of the French national library. The miniature opposite suggests a good deal about Charles's temperament. The artist-courtier who painted it felt free to depict quite unflatteringly the king's long pointed nose, but he presented him in the robes of an astrologer, that is, a serious student of astronomical science.

Charles V, opposite, receives an illuminated Bible from his adviser Jean de Vaudetar. The miniature appears as the frontispiece of that Bible.

A lavish host, the fur-hatted Duc de Berry sits at table surrounded by his feasting courtiers in a miniature by Pol de Limbourg representing the month of January in the Très Riches Heures.

JEAN, DUC DE BERRY

HIS BOOK OF HOURS

A self-confidant connoisseur with a taste for the exquisite, an art collector with an insatiable appetite, Jean, Duc de Berry, has had few peers as a patron of the arts. Indeed, his patronage was so extensive that he left his personal mark on the art of his age. The elegant decorative style known as the International Style was to a great extent fostered by de Berry in his role as director and monopolizer of whole teams of fine artists. The nineteenth-century French poets who celebrated decadent aestheticism and self-indulgent dandyhood might well have harked back to de Berry as their model. Here was an extravagant aristocrat who, among other conceits, kept live bears in his retinue when he traveled between his seventeen houses and who once kept a young girl captive in one of his castles to oblige an artist who was in love with her. To pay for his munificence, de Berry so oppressed the province of Languedoc that Charles VI had to take it away from him for the sake of civil peace. Yet it is not with decadence but with artistic renewal that de Berry's name is deservedly associated. The brothers Limbourg, who illuminated for him a Book of Hours called the *Très Riches Heures*, were the first to effectively incorporate into northern European art the concept of perspective. The *Très Riches Heures* of the Duc de Berry, shown in these pages, marks a turning point in the history of painting.

The influence of the zodiac on various bodily parts is gracefully symbolized in the Très Riches Heures.

The Garden of Eden, opposite page, is an exquisite toy world, and Adam and Eve are refined and winsome, in the Limbourgs' rendering of the Fall for the Duc de Berry.

Satan spews up the damned with his fiery breath while demons work the realistic bellows of an infernal forge in the Limbourgs' picture of Hell in the Très Riches Heures.

THE ROYAL CUP
OF ENGLAND AND FRANCE

The Royal Gold Cup of the kings of England and France, shown above, is one of the few surviving relics of the Duc de Berry's golden treasure-trove. Studded with pearls, it is decorated with a translucent enamel painting, right, that depicts the life of Saint Agnes, who was burned at the stake about A.D. 305. Because Saint Agnes was Charles V's patron saint, the cup is believed to have been made originally for him. In 1434 the Duke of Bedford seized it as war booty, and his nephew Henry VI later inherited it. When the cup passed through the hands of England's Tudor kings, its stem was adorned with the Tudor rose emblem, one reason, perhaps, why the first Stuart king, James I, gave it away to a Spaniard soon after his accession. In 1892 the British Museum acquired it from a French family, by which time the much-traveled, and much-ornamented, cup had lost several of its precious sapphires, rubies, and pearls.

LOUIS, DUKE OF ANJOU

"And the third angel sounded, and there fell a great star from heaven . . . And the name of the star is called "Wormword."

HIS ANGERS APOCALYPSE

As a patron of art, Louis, Duke of Anjou, lagged behind his brothers. If the new courtly art they favored tended at times toward ostentation, this defect was strongest in Louis's patronage. It is not his collection of more than three thousand gold and silver objects but his ownership of silver kitchenware that reveals his rule of taste. The rule, in general, was that any object that could be made in a precious metal should be, and any surface that could be decorated should be laden with ornament. Whereas his brothers had their books illustrated with superb miniatures, Louis had decorations adorning his eating utensils, which were usually of gold. None of the Duke's golden tableware survives, partly because of Louis himself. It is recorded that one of his goldsmiths became a hermit after the Duke melted down all his creations to raise funds. Still the Duke of Anjou can claim a peerless distinction as an art patron: he commissioned one of the masterpieces of medieval art. This is a sequence of huge tapestries illustrating in some ninety scenes the Book of Revelation, or the Apocalypse, the last book of the New Testament. The Angers tapestries (seen opposite and on pages 71–77) are the oldest, the largest, and perhaps the finest examples of this type of weaving to survive.

70

"And I saw a woman sit upon a scarlet coloured beast, full of names of blasphemy, having seven heads and ten horns.

"And the shapes of the locusts were like unto horses prepared unto battle; and on their heads were as it were crowns like gold

and their faces were as the faces of men. . . . And they had a king over them, which is the angel of the bottomless pit . . .''

"And there was war in heaven: Michael and his angels fought against the dragon; and the dragon fought and hi.

angels, And prevailed not; neither was their place found any more in heaven. And the great dragon was cast out . . .''

"And he cried mightily with a strong voice, saying, Babylon the great is fallen, is fallen, and is become the habitation of devils, and the hol

f every foul spirit, and a cage of every unclean and hateful bird. For all nations have drunk of the wine of the wrath of her fornication . . .''

PHILIP THE BOLD, DUKE OF BURGUNDY

The dazzlingly ornate tomb of Philip the Bold was begun by Claus Sluter in 1383, some twenty years before the Duke's death.

HIS TOMB AND THE WELL OF MOSES

In his unabashed love of opulent display, Philip the Bold, Duke of Burgundy, not only out-matched his brothers but initiated a tradition that long made the Burgundian court a byword for extravagance. One source of that extravagance was a literary ideal, for Philip was guided by those tales of chivalry and conventions of knightly romance to which all the Valois brothers were devoted. In a sense they were bent on creating a mode of courtly life that had never existed except in the ballads of troubadours and the tales of the romancers, but they took it seriously nonetheless. Perhaps this is one reason why Philip and his brothers were such extraordinarily munificent patrons of the arts. They urgently needed the vast tapestries, the ornate jewelry, gold utensils, luxuriant clothing, illuminated prayer books, and elaborate castles in order to create that environment of elegance that was inseparable from the fantasies of chivalry they were trying to bring to life. Interestingly, however, it was through the far more traditional motive of religious piety that Philip the Bold is best remembered in the history of art. When he commissioned his resident artist, Claus Sluter, to design a lavish tomb (above), and erect a huge, ornamented crucifix (its base is shown on the opposite page), for a Carthusian monastery, he gave the gifted Dutch artist an unparalleled opportunity to create two masterpieces of fourteenth-century sculpture. In the end no art patron can do more than that.

Philip's gift to the Carthusians included Sluter's great Well of Moses, opposite, adorned with statues of prophets.

You Can Take
A Boy Out of Dunfermline…

At home in Scotland, Carnegie sports native tweeds, and the obligatory collie, beside an ivied wall at Skibo, his mountain retreat in Sutherlandshire.

In railways, steel, and finance Andrew Carnegie was a cool, rational man. And his venture into charity in his own home-town was meant to be "scientific," too— but underlying it all was a warm, unreasoning passion

By JOSEPH FRAZIER WALL

In 1889 Andrew Carnegie, in his usual bold and provocative manner, stated his philosophy of philanthropy. His article "Wealth," in the *North American Review,* created a considerable stir, for people are always interested in men who have money, and they are doubly fascinated by those who announce that they intend to give it away. W. T. Stead, the editor of the *Pall Mall Gazette,* reprinted the article for the British public under a new title, "The Gospel of Wealth," which was quickly accepted on both sides of the Atlantic. Carnegie, who was always uncomfortable around people who preached gospels, would have preferred a different title, for he regarded his statement as an objective appraisal of the "proper administration of wealth." Just as Marx had regarded all socialists who preceded him as starry-eyed idealists whose utopian fantasies must give way to his "scientific socialism," so Carnegie felt that he was providing America's rapidly growing millionaire class with a meaningful prescription for "scientific philanthropy," thus bringing discipline and purpose to the simple random distribution of largess, which usually did more harm than good.

It would be far better, Carnegie believed, to "throw one's money into the sea" than to give it to that "submerged tenth of the population...the irreclaimably distitute, shiftless, and worthless." The head must rule the philanthropist, not the heart. In response to a letter from an acquaintance in Pittsburgh who criticized him for "not giving with his heart as well as his head," Carnegie answered, "My friend, the heart is the steam in the boiler; the head is the engine that regulates dangerous steam and prevents disastrous explosions. So far from my heart being allowed to more control, I see that wisdom requires it to be more and more repressed."

In one major instance, however, Carnegie clearly did allow his heart to control his head. Dunfermline, his beloved native town in Scotland, was to provide Carnegie with a way of letting off steam. It served as a safety valve for sentiment, for which he would never make an apology.

Carnegie had already made generous gifts to his native town, having provided it with his first library and with swimming baths that were the marvel of Scotland. Dunfermline, in return, had given to its most illustrious living son his first "freedom of the city." Carnegie was eager to do more, much more, for the "auld grey toon." It was the classic case of the returning son who, having achieved fame and fortune elsewhere, became prodigal at home because he felt it still necessary to prove himself in a place where he had once been a nobody. Carnegie's proof was to exceed all expectations.

It all began in 1900, when Colonel Thomas Hunt, the Laird of Pittencrieff, approached John Ross, Carnegie's Dunfermline solicitor, with the rather surprising suggestion that he might be willing to sell the Pittencrieff estate if Carnegie would meet his price. Ross was amazed at this suggestion, for like all citizens of Dunfermline he knew of the old feud between the Hunt and Morrison families. Colonel Hunt's father, James Hunt, had for half a century carried on a running court battle with old Tom Morrison, Carnegie's grandfather, and with his son, Bailie Morrison, over the rights of the people of Dunfermline vs. the rights of the lairds of Pittencrieff. The Hunts were relative newcomers to the landed gentry class of Scotland. Grandfather Morrison had known men who remembered the time when James Hunt's grandfather had earned an honest living as a barber in Dunfermline. But having acquired some wealth through fortunate investments, the Hunts had purchased Pittencrieff, at the edge of the city, and were constantly trying to enlarge their estate by encroaching upon the common lands of the town. The Morrisons, who always enjoyed a public lawsuit, had on several occasions brought James Hunt to court and had successfully blocked his efforts at ex-

pansion. They had also forced him to open his estate once a year in order that the historic monuments in the Glen of Pittencrieff might be viewed by the public. After one such suit, the enraged Hunt had challenged Bailie Morrison to a duel, a challenge that was quickly accepted. "All right," boomed out Andrew's Uncle Tom for all the town to hear, "I'll fight ye. As challenged party I have the choice of weapons. I'll take my father's shoemaker's knife and you take your grandfather's razor."

Such insults were not quickly forgotten, and James Hunt had decreed that thereafter no Morrison or descendant of a Morrison should ever step foot on Pittencrieff's sacred soil. Like a fabled ogre, James Hunt stood at the entrance to the estate on the one day of the year that the glen was open to the public to make sure that no Morrison got inside—and that included the small boy Andrew, barred by his ancestry from seeing those historic ruins of Dunfermline's glorious past that lay inside Pittencrieff's gates: King Malcolm's tower, Margaret's shrine, and the one remaining wall of the palace of the Stuarts. Now, sixty years later, James Hunt's son was offering to sell all of it to that same Andrew, thus making old Tom Morrison's grandson the Laird of Pittencrieff. Hunt's price was £70,000, which Ross, in writing to Carnegie about the offer, thought was double what it was worth. "I cannot conceive what has put selling into the Colonel's head. I thought he would never part with the Park & the Glen." After consulting with Carnegie, Ross told Hunt that the price was too high and that Mr. Carnegie was not disposed to consider the purchase further.

But of course Carnegie *was* disposed to consider the matter further. There was nothing in the world he wanted quite as much as Pittencrieff. The negotiations continued for more than two years, with Lord Shaw of Dunfermline, who was on much better terms with the Hunt family than was Ross,

acting as Carnegie's intermediary. Finally, on Christmas Eve, 1902, Carnegie purchased for himself the most wonderful Christmas present of his life, the entire Pittencrieff estate—for £45,000. To Cousin Dod, his uncle George Lauder's son, he simply wrote, *"Pittencrieff is ours."* No need to tell his boyhood companion what the possession of Pittencrieff meant to Andrew. To his friend John Morley, Carnegie wrote more explicitly:

My new title beats all. I am Laird of Pittencrieff—that's the glen & Palace ruins at Dunfermline, the most sacred spot to me on Earth. Would rather be Pittencrieff than King Edward by a long shot. I laugh at the importance of it. It really tickles me. But Oh—those who have passed should be here to enjoy it. What it would have meant to my Grandfather, Father, Uncles. Ah, Uncle Lauder more than any. He was born in Pittencrieff Glen & played on its sunny braes as a child.

Clearly, Carnegie was in the proper sentimental mood to make a handsome benefaction to Dunfermline, and Pittencrieff was to be the first installment. In November, 1903, with formal solemn rites, which Carnegie, who was in New York, could not attend, the estate was transferred in perpetuity to the Royal Burgh of Dunfermline. Carnegie kept for himself during his lifetime the small portion of the estate that included the mound upon which the ruins of Malcolm's tower rested, just above the point where the small creek, or linn, made the bend that gave Dunfermline its name. Keeping this bit of land allowed Carnegie to retain his proud new title, Laird of Pittencrieff.

Carnegie asked Lord Shaw to be his representative at the formal opening of Pittencrieff. "If it were practicable to associate with you my cousin, Robert Morrison, I think it will be a fine touch. You know his father, Bailie Morrison, is to be credited with getting part of the ruins back to the nation and open to Dunfermline. The then Mr. Hunt, by special order, prohibited any Morrison from entering them. To have his son stand in Pittencrieff at your side and to be a party to presenting the whole estate to Dunfermline would be historically fine."

John Ross wrote a long letter to Carnegie the day after Pittencrieff was opened as a public park. As is so often true of Dunfermline in November, the weather had been bad for several days, and on the morning of the ceremony there were showers. "Then it became so beautiful that you could not have failed to believe in a Special Providence. Never since the Park was created has it looked better, never was there a more lovely sunset, a clearer view, a lovelier moon . . . Lord Elgin and his two daughters headed the procession, then came a carriage with Mr. & Mrs. Shaw and Mr. & Mrs. Morrison . . . The Lauders were under the escort of Hew Morrison in full Highland costume. I must not forget to say that costume was the order of the day. I was ablaze in a scarlet robe. The wonder is I did not take fire . . . Ah me! when shall we see the like of that procession again?"

From the time of the inaugural ceremonies, the gates have been opened every day of the year, and it is truly a park for the people. A concert hall and tearoom were built in the center of the park, along with great conservatories that brought the flamboyant beauty of the tropics to this unlikely old gray town on the cold Firth of Forth. Majestic peacocks now sweep their tails across Pittencrieff's vast lawns, while with equal incongruity, the drab native sparrows flutter through the glass-enclosed tropics of the conservatories, luxuriating in the warmth as they pick up the seeds of exotic jungle plants.

Pittencrieff was but a part, though to Carnegie a very special part, of a much larger plan he had in mind for Dunfermline. During the summer of 1903, while the old Hunt estate was being cleaned up and landscaped for its opening, Carnegie was busy with Ross drafting a deed that would create the Carnegie Dunfermline Trust. As a preamble to it, Carnegie had written:

I, Andrew Carnegie of New York and of Skibo in the County of Sutherland, Scotland in pursuance of a duty which I have long felt incumbent on me and which I have so far already endeavored to discharge, vizt: —to distribute in my lifetime the surplus wealth which I possess in such a manner as shall best advance the well-being and happiness of the greatest number of beneficiaries; and being desirous of testing by experiment the advantages which a community may derive by having placed at its disposal, under the administration of public spirited and intelligent men chosen from among themselves, funds dedicated to the purpose of providing the means of introducing into the daily lives of the masses, such privileges and enjoyments as are under present circumstances considered beyond their reach, but which if brought within their reach are calculated to carry into their homes and their conduct sweetness and light . . .

It is interesting to note that in the first draft of the deed, Carnegie attempted to cover his sentimentality with a cloak of rationality, so that he might still appear before the world as the "scientific philanthropist." He had carefully made the point that he was bestowing these riches upon Dunfermline "from no partiality to my native town" but rather as a part of a larger scientific experiment in which he intended to select a town of equal size in the United States to which he would also bring the gifts of "sweetness and light." Fortunately for Carnegie's sanity this was deleted in the final draft, for one can imagine the flood of applications from towns all over the United States putting forth claims to be part of the experiment. Carnegie was obliged to appear as an unabashed sentimentalist.

In the earlier drafts Carnegie had also been quite specific as to the areas of "sweetness and light" in which he expected the trustees to be active: public gardens, parks, golf links, art galleries, public exhibitions of art, lecturers, public entertainment such as theatrical and musical events, musical societies, field trips for schoolchildren to historic and scenic spots in Scotland, the restoration of the abbey and palace in Dunfermline, medical clinics, even model hous-

ing for the poor. These specific proposals were also deleted in the final draft, and instead Carnegie charged the trustees with the undefined task of bringing "into the monotonous lives of the toiling masses of Dunfermline more of sweetness and light; to give to them—especially the young—some charm, some happiness, some elevating conditions of life which residence elsewhere would have denied; that the child of my native town, looking back in after years, however far from home it may have roamed, will feel that simply by virtue of being such, life has been made happier and better. . . . Remember you are pioneers . . . Try many things freely, but discard just as freely . . ."

Carnegie had granted considerable freedom of action to the trustees of all his philanthropic trusts, but in no other did he take such a personal interest. For weeks he fussed with Ross, who was the designated chairman, over the selection of the other trustees. Carnegie had wanted a Roman Catholic priest as a member of the commission, but this was too ecumenical for Calvinist Dunfermline. Ross, in as polite a way as possible, informed Carnegie that in his opinion "no priest would care to serve and the Roman Catholics in Dunfermline would not feel such a representation necessary." Carnegie yielded: "All right, Boss. Exit Holy Father, but I like to keep in with one who can really grant absolution. It may be handy someday." On one point, however, Carnegie was adamant. There had to be representatives of the working class on the commission along with the more wealthy business and professional men and town and county officials. So John Weir, Secretary of the Fife Miners Union; John Hynd, a miner; and James Brown, a dyer, were there with the Beveridges, the Earl of Elgin, and Provost James Macbeth.

Carnegie also had definite ideas about projects, even though the specification of those projects had been taken out of the deed. As he became increasingly liberal in his political views, in reconciliation with his radical origins, this progressivism was reflected in his philanthropic ideas. In 1911 he wrote Ross that he wanted him to look into the possibility of "model housing for the poor." Remembering his own childhood days of squabbling with neighborhood women over the use of the town pump, he said he wanted to make sure that these houses had indoor plumbing, especially a bathroom. "I consider this the most important feature . . . I know of no way of diffusing sweetness and lite more easily and practically than by improving housing conditions among the poor." Again, Ross felt obliged to set Carnegie straight on the facts of life. "Where is this experiment to stop? If the Trust began they would at once create antagonism with all the present house owners, who would say that they were being subjected to an unfair competition, and there would be no possibility of satisfying the demands of those who would wish to inhabit the model houses . . . I quite agree that the improvement of houses for the poorer classes is one of the most urgent social needs, but it is a complex question and involves a good many others, such as the wages which the tenants earn out of which the rent must be paid. It involves also the social habits of the people and their ability to do justice to the occupation of such houses."

Carnegie was disappointed. "The tone of yours of March 9th is indeed discouraging." But he was not ready to yield completely: "Here is a suggestion submitted for discussion by one entirely ignorant of the situation, but therefore certain he is right as usual in this." Carnegie's suggestion was for the trust to approach the owners saying that it would fix up houses for the tenants if the owners would not then charge any more rent. The trustees gave as scant attention to this modification as they had to the original proposal. Britain was not yet ready for the welfare state, even if done by private philanthropy.

On the other hand, sharp disagreement arose on occasion between Carnegie and the trustees when they proposed projects that ran counter to his views. His most acrimonious dispute with Ross came over a proposal to build an extension for the Dunfermline library, which, since it was his first library, he regarded with proprietary interest. Carnegie got the idea that the extension was to be used only as a special research library for scholars, and this he vigorously objected to because it did not contribute to the welfare of "the toiling masses." If scholars wanted a library for research, they could go to Edinburgh. It reached the point where Ross, in exasperation, wrote a very strong letter to Carnegie, which Carnegie may have destroyed, for it is not in his papers. Carnegie replied in that tone of long-suffering martyrdom that his business partners knew so well:

You surely regret the words you have riten me but I forgive you . . . Has it come to this, that I cannot be permitted to forcibly express my feelings? I have had and am having as much experience as you with Libraries for the Masses which is what I consider most important. Libraries for antiquarians are within reach of Dunfermline as I point out—not for working man as you have it. My Friend, beware of the weaknesses of old age—which as I begin to learn from experience sometimes betray us into regretful words or action against those we love and honor most. I have laid aside your letter, sad, indeed, feeling that I have not deserved at your hands such a blow—not angry, no, no—but oh so sorry.

At this point the vice-chairman of the trust, Sir William Robertson, jumped into the fray and told Carnegie bluntly that his stand reflected on the judgment and good sense of the trustees. He said that the extension was not just for the use of antiquaries. The library had outgrown its present facilities and he for one felt they needed an entirely new building. Under such pressure, Carnegie yielded and agreed to £5,000 being spent for an extension. He would, he said placatingly, let the trustees decide on the plans—"nothing too good

for their reward here or hereafter."

Considering the restrictions under which they worked, the trustees did a remarkable job over the years in dispensing "sweetness and light" to the fortunate citizens of Dunfermline. The income from the trust, originally endowed at two and a half million dollars but soon raised to four million, amounted to $200,000 annually, making Dunfermline, a town of 27,000, the community with the largest private endowment in the world.

Within a decade the trust had managed to make Pittencrieff into one of the most beautiful parks in all Britain; had built new swimming baths, a gymnasium, a College of Hygiene, and a clinic that provided medical and dental care for all the children of the town; had established a school for the training of physical education teachers for all of Scotland, a school of music providing free music lessons to all Dunfermline children wishing to participate, a school of horticulture, a Women's Institute for training in homemaking and vocational skills; and had set up free tours of Scotland for schoolchildren, financed a full concert series on an annual basis, and provided lectures and theatrical productions for the town. Carnegie had reason enough to write Chairman Ross and the members of the Dunfermline trust in 1914, not long before his last visit to his native city: "You have fulfilled the hope I indulged—the child of Dunfermline looking back will realize that 'birth in Dunfermline has given advantages which birth elsewhere would have denied.' Be of good cheer, you labor not for flattering reward from your townsmen, but from your own conscience which tells you that because you have lived and labored, the people of Dunfermline have been advantaged—glorious work this."

Joseph Frazier Wall is Parker Professor of History and Dean of Grinnell College. This article is taken from his book Andrew Carnegie, *to be published this fall by Oxford University Press.*

The Battle of the Nile

This fashionable portrait of Nelson was done by Lemuel Abbott. Of his famous command ships painted by Nicholas Pocock, the Victory, *of Trafalgar fame, is at right, and the* Vanguard, *flagship in the Battle of the Nile, is second from left.*

Napoleon's ships drifted helplessly at anchor;
Lord Nelson boldly closed on them, improvising
his tactics as he bore down on the French fleet.
Nelson was victorious, as was his habit, and
with the victory came British control of the
Mediterranean for more than a hundred years

The French Revolutionary and Napoleonic wars, lasting from 1792 to 1815, were fought on the battlefields of Europe, on the great oceans of the world, and on the Mediterranean Sea. It was here, indeed, that disaster overtook Napoleon, when his expedition to Egypt was shattered by the loss of his whole fleet in the Battle of the Nile. Whereas on land the revolutionary ardor of the French nation was at one time or another turned against almost every nation in Europe, at sea the conflict was largely between two nations, England and France. In the end, although Napoleon's ambitions were terminated on the field of Waterloo, the struggle at sea decided the issue and determined the course of the century that was to follow. As with Carthage and Rome, it was a battle between leviathan and behemoth, a sea empire confronting a land empire, a nation of merchants and traders fighting against a nation of hardy peasant farmers. In this case—and only because the British, unlike the Carthaginians, did not forget that their existence depended upon mastery of the sea—the issue was differently resolved. Napoleon, war lord, lawgiver, and statesman, had as great a dislike of the sea as any ancient Roman. Lord Nelson, on the other hand, only faltered when he stepped ashore.

Behold the man-of-war, the sailing ship of the line, which swept the Mediterranean from the Strait of Gibraltar to the Levant. The ship comes proudly driving toward us, as she soars, lifts, and falters over the uneasy swell of the Bay of Biscay. Bound for the Mediterranean theatre of war, she looks as beautiful and assured as any sea bird. Whether English or French, her composition differed only in minor points —frequently, when it came to design and manning, to the advantage of the French. Good though the English naval architects were, the French were often their superiors, and as for the methods of manning their vessels, the French were certainly more intelligent. The

French, for example, gave special pay to their fishermen to induce them to train and learn in the equivalent to a naval reserve. The English, on the other hand, still depended largely upon "pressed men"—forcibly conscripted sailors—to man what Admiral Mahan has described as "those far-distant, storm-beaten ships, upon which the Grand Army never looked, but which for ever stood between it and the dominion of the World."

Present in the Mediterranean during the Revolutionary and Napoleonic wars was the most famous warship in history, H.M.S. *Victory*. Since she was in many respects typical of the great ships of the line that were to dominate the sea until the advent of steam, some description of her, and of life aboard her, may help to set the scene for certain events of the late eighteenth and early nineteenth centuries. Launched at Old Single Dock, Chatham, Kent, in 1765, the *Victory* was the fifth ship of the Royal Navy to bear that name. The first had been the flagship of Sir John Hawkins in the Armada campaign of 1588. That Elizabethan galleon had displaced 560 tons, but the new *Victory,* fairly typical of other large ships of the line, was registered at 2,162 tons —although it has been estimated that she displaced nearer 3,500.

This ship, of which Thackeray said, "the bones of the *Victory* ought to be sacred relics for Englishmen to worship," was built chiefly of English oak and elm. Her hull was more than two feet thick; her sternpost was made of one huge oak tree, and much of the wood used in her construction came from trees that were at least a hundred years old. Her keel—more than 150 feet long—was made of teak, one of the hardest and most worm-resistant woods in the world, and this again was protected by a false keel of elm. Her fastenings consisted of oak pins, known as trennels, and copper bolts six feet long and two inches in diameter. Both in her materials and in the weight of her construction, she was something that no Mediterranean shipbuilder of

the past could ever have conceived of.

Her complement was upwards of 850 men, and she had sufficient water and provisions to stay at sea for four months, while she carried enough powder and shot to last her—short of some major action—three years. The most remarkable feature of these giant sailing ships was the enormous weight of metal they carried, for by now it was well understood that the broadside determined battles, and indeed, the fate of empires. A ship like the *Victory* was known as a three-decker, after her three gun decks (there were, in fact, seven different levels on such a vessel). A ship of this kind was a floating gun platform: the lower gun deck carried the heaviest guns, 32-pounders; the middle carried 24-pounders; and the upper, 12-pounders.

The term broadside—of which so much has been written both in history and in fiction—did not mean that all the guns on one side were fired at the same moment. Strong though these ships were, they could never have withstood such a concussion. "Ripple firing," whereby the guns were fired consecutively from forward to aft, was what took place during a broadside action. By the time the afterguns were firing, the forward guns were all reloaded and ready to repeat the "ripple" fire. The upper gun deck aimed at the enemy's masts and rigging, while the two lower decks sought to blow her sides to pieces. Such actions, sometimes lasting for a number of hours, were about the bloodiest and most murderous in the whole history of warfare at sea.

Much has been said about the condition of the men who manned the galleys of the Mediterranean during this and earlier periods. The expression "like a galley slave" has passed into the English language to indicate almost insupportable toil, but the fact remains that—although he was theoretically a free man—the life of a sailor aboard a great ship of the line was as hard as any galley slave's. "Wooden ships need

By ERNLE BRADFORD

85

Four by Thomas Rowlandson: a purser

iron men" was hardly an exaggeration.

A large number of the seamen aboard the *Victory* and her sister ships in the Royal Navy had been forcibly pressed into service. The Vagrancy Act laid down that "all disreputable persons" (which might mean anyone found in a tavern, let alone a bawdyhouse, or even walking peaceably down the streets of a fishing port) were liable for impressment. So were fishermen, merchant seamen, and canalmen or inland watermen—if they were unfortunate enough to be caught by the press gang. Since so large a percentage of a ship's company was forcibly conscripted, discipline aboard had to be of an iron-bound severity. The citizens of England who manned Her Majesty's ships during the Napoleonic wars were ill-clad, ill-used, and to a large extent, unwilling, seamen.

Some indication of the sailor's lot can be gauged from a book published during this period, called *Nautical Economy; or, Forecastle Recollections of Events during the last War. Dedicated to the Brave Tars of Old England by a Sailor, politely called by the officers of the Navy, Jack Nasty-Face.* Even allowing for the fact that "Jack" was a deeply embittered man, there can be little denying the truth of his account, for it is substantiated by a number of others. "Out of a fleet of nine sail of the line I was with," he wrote, "there were only two captains thus distinguished [for their humanity]. They kept order on board without resorting to the frequent and unnecessary call upon the boatswain and his cat, adopted by the other seven; and what was the consequence? Those two ships beat us in reefing and furling; for they were not in fear and dread, well knowing they would not be punished without a real and just cause."

Jack goes on to describe the discipline that prevailed aboard those "storm-beaten ships": "The cat-of-nine-tails is applied to the bare back, and at about every six lashes a fresh boatswain's mate is ordered to relieve the executioner of this duty, until the prisoner has received, perhaps, twenty-five lashes . . . [He is] conveyed from ship to ship, receiving alongside of each a similar number of stripes with the cat until his sentence is completed. . . . his back resembles so much putrified liver, and every stroke of the cat brings away the congealed blood; and the boatswain's mates are looked at with the eye of a hawk to see they do their duty, and clear the cat's tails after every stroke, the blood at the time streaming through their fingers: and in this manner are men in the navy punished for different offences, more particularly impressed men who attempt to make their escape." This was the world of the human machinery that fought the *Victory*'s canvas in a gale or her guns in action—the ship so beautiful to the outward eye as she buried the green rollers of the sea beneath her dolphin striker and stumbled toward Cape Trafalgar over the awkward Biscay swell.

Nelson himself was one of the few commanders of his time who tried to improve the conditions of his sailors. He might well have been one of those two captains whom Jack describes as keeping order on board without resorting to "the boatswain and his cat." Apart from being a genius as a sailor, Nelson was a sensitive man. He knew —as Drake had known centuries before him—that the seaman is every whit as entitled to fair and reasonable conditions as any other man. Since his captains, whom he called his "Band of Brothers," always sought to emulate him, Nelson no doubt played a large part in improving the lot of the British seaman.

The food of these men was simple enough. Breakfast "usually consists of burgoo, made of coarse oatmeal and water; others will have Scotch coffee, which is burnt bread boiled in some water, and sweetened with sugar." At noon, "the pleasantest part of the day . . . every man and boy is allowed a pint, that is, one gill of rum and three of water, to which is added lemon acid, sweetened with sugar." The main dish consisted of salt beef or pork with pease pudding, and for supper "half a pint of wine, or a pint of grog, to each man, with biscuit, and cheese or butter." Life aboard may have been hard, the discipline harsh, but the food in general compared favorably with that of the country laborer of the time. And the sailor always had the chance of winning some prize money.

The whole ship existed to serve the guns. In the sight, smell, service, and thunder of them the sailor lived and died. The *Victory*'s true and indomi-

A midshipman with book and implements

A sailor with a seagoing appetite

table face was revealed as soon as she stripped for action. Even the comparatively elegant quarters of the admiral were denuded of their furniture and gear, which was sent down to the main hold below the water line. From the lower deck, where the majority of the seamen slept and fed, the men's hammocks were taken up top and lashed along the bulwarks to serve as protection against flying splinters and the bullets of enemy marksmen. (A high proportion of the casualties suffered in action was caused by splinters of wood gouged out of the ships' decks and sides by cannon balls.)

The men fought the guns, stripped to the waist, with a handkerchief tied around their forehead and ears to keep the sweat out of their eyes and to protect their ears against the deafening thunder of the guns. They worked barefoot, and the decks were swilled with sea water to reduce the risk of fire, as well as sprinkled with sand to prevent the sailors from slipping. The mortally wounded and the dead were thrown overboard without ceremony. Those whose wounds were within the limited capacity of the surgeons were taken down to the afterpart of the orlop deck, the cockpit. This area was painted red so the wounded would not notice how much of that red was their own blood. There were no anesthetics, and major

operations were undertaken either by stunning the patient or, if time permitted, by getting him blind drunk on brandy or rum. As often as not, the strong arms of the surgeon's mates held the wounded down. The same hot pitch that served to calk the ship's seams was used to seal amputations, while gunpowder, sea salt, and brandy or rum were used as primitive antiseptics.

The officers could expect no more than the men if they had the misfortune to be wounded. Nelson himself, who in a lifetime of action had lost both an arm and the sight of an eye, could hope for no better medical attention than that given to the humblest ordinary seaman. It was a hard life and it bred hard men, but that they were not necessarily insensitive is proved by Nelson among many others. The sea life has always had its compensations, and many sailors retained a vein of poetry that their rough exteriors belied. As one commander wrote to his wife: "To be sure I lose the fruits of the earth, but then I am gathering the flowers of the sea."

The wars with revolutionary France, in which Britain was strong at sea but militarily weak, dragged on for many years. The focus sharpened upon the Mediterranean theatre in 1793, when a young British naval captain, Horatio Nelson, who had been, in the phrase, "on the beach" for five years, received a new seagoing appointment. As he wrote his wife: "The Admiralty so smile upon me, that really I am as much surprised as when they frowned. Lord Chatham yesterday made many apologies for not having given me a Ship before this time, and said, that if I chose to take a Sixty-four to begin with, I should be appointed to one as soon as she was ready; and whenever it was in his power, I should be removed into a Seventy-four. Everything indicates War. One of our ships, looking into Brest, has been fired into."

The 64-gun ship of the line to which Nelson was appointed as captain was

the *Agamemnon*—a name appropriate enough to the Mediterranean, whither she was immediately dispatched under the command of Admiral Hood. Aided by French Royalists, the British fleet enjoyed an immediate success, capturing the great port and naval base of Toulon, which was shortly retaken by the French revolutionary forces—prominent among whose officers was a young commander of the artillery named Napoleon Bonaparte. The following year, 1794, during the siege of Calvi in Corsica, Nelson lost the sight of his right eye when a shot from the French garrison landed near the battery where he was engaged, throwing up a mass of sand and splinters that struck him in the face. There is an erroneous belief that he always wore a patch over this damaged eye, but in fact the eye looked perfectly normal.

During these years, while he was learning to become, as he later put it, "An old Mediterranean man," his duties were similar to those of dozens of other sea captains engaged around the French coast, or off Corsica and Sardinia, or in the long stretches of sea west of Sicily. British convoys had to be protected, contraband runners had to be intercepted, and there was sometimes an occasional brush with the enemy. But in the main the sailor's time was spent in long, frustrating days

A ship's cook at work in the galley

The sailors' tipple, grog, was rationed; often, as in George Cruikshank's etching above, it inspired a song. Officers, however, could drink their fill of port, and—as Rowlandson's caricature below attests—did.

at sea, with the ship's bottom growing foul in the warm water and the sun-baked ropes and canvas chafing and fraying in idle weather, or blowing away in one of the sudden and fierce storms typical of the area. After one engagement, in which Nelson had distinguished himself by capturing the huge 84-gun *Ca Ira* with his 64-gun *Agamemnon,* he confessed in a letter to his wife: "I wish to be an Admiral, and in command of the English fleet; I should very soon either do much, or be ruined: my disposition cannot bear tame and slow measures."

Another whose disposition could not bear "tame and slow measures" was the great Corsican, who was soon to take the French Revolution all over Europe and the East. At the age of twenty-six Bonaparte, already a general, had entered Italy with an army of about forty thousand half-starved soldiers in want of everything except the fire and spirit that their revolutionary fervor had kindled within them. In words that might have been spoken long centuries before by Hannibal, he addressed them as follows: "You are badly fed and all but naked. . . . I am

about to lead you into the most fertile plains in the world. Before you are great cities and rich provinces; there we shall find honour, glory, and riches."

His promises were soon fulfilled, the Italian people hailing him as the man who liberated them from their Austrian masters. All over Europe nations were welcoming the new ideas of revolutionary France that were bursting open the old wineskins of royalist and feudal centuries. Czarist Russia, for obvious reasons, was hostile, while England was anxious not only about the threat to her own security that a united Europe might pose but also about the threat to her overseas empire. Having lost the Thirteen Colonies, England's great concern now was India, and Napoleon was already looking in that direction. Beyond Italy lay the sea route to Egypt, and beyond Egypt lay all the wealth of the East.

Napoleon embodied, in his concept of his mission, all the dreams of his great predecessors. He had, first of all, a vision of restoring the ancient Roman Empire. The whole of the Mediterranean area, Italy, Spain, Egypt, and the adjacent countries of the Levant, should be united within one framework under the dominance of France. Napoleon saw himself as the Caesar of this new empire, but he also dreamed of being an Alexander. Beyond a united Mediterranean he looked eastward, as had the great Macedonian, and it was this aspect of his nature that alarmed the English more than anything else. Had Napoleon confined his actions to the Continent, the English might possibly, if unwillingly, have accepted the imperial *fait accompli.* But the threat to their great Eastern empire was something they could never tolerate.

While Italy was being turned into a block of republics on the French model, Napoleon's eyes were fixed upon the islands lying to the south of him. He regarded them as steppingstones to the East. Since fertile and fruitful Sicily was barred to him by the sun-bleached canvases, the oak hulls, and the 32-pounders of the Royal Navy, he looked farther southward and saw in Malta, as so many had seen before him, the perfect harbor from which to dominate the Mediterranean. It would be some years, however, before he would make a move in that direction—years in which the French were everywhere successful on land and in which the British tried as far as possible to contain them by sea. But by the latter part of 1796 the British position in the Mediterranean had clearly become untenable—for the moment, at any rate. The French were masters of the Continent; and keeping three fleets in being—one in the Mediterranean, another based at Gibraltar and Portugal (England's only ally at the time), and the third at the western approaches to the Channel—was straining English resources.

The British therefore withdrew to Gibraltar, their one secure fortress and the key to control of the sea gates. Not long after this, in an unsuccessful attack on Tenerife in the Canary Islands, Nelson (by now an admiral) lost his right arm, which was taken off at the elbow after he was hit by grapeshot. He was convinced that his career was over, that only retirement lay ahead, and that he would never more command the ships of England against the French, for whom he felt a passionate hatred. Curiously enough, Nelson never seems to have disliked his Spanish opponents, often, indeed, expressing his admiration for them. But he hated the French and everything they stood for, which, to his conservative nature, seemed to be the destruction of all law, order, and decency.

He wrote at this time to his commander in chief, Earl St. Vincent: "I am become a burthen to my friends and useless to my Country. When I leave your command, I become dead to the world; I go hence and am no more seen." To this St. Vincent replied: "Mortals cannot command success. You and your companions have certainly deserved it, by the greatest degree of heroism and perseverance that ever was exhibited." At that moment in time neither man could have foreseen that within a year the British would be back in force in the Mediterranean, let alone that within a year Nelson would have gained one of the most outstanding victories ever to take place on that sea.

Napoleon, in the meantime, had come to realize that the French fleet was in no state to carry out the great invasion of England that had been planned. Large-scale invasion of the arrogant island was still the dream of the French Republic, but Napoleon was wise enough to see that it must be deferred. The immediate aim must be to strike in the East in order to threaten India. To achieve this objective, an immense fleet and army must be assembled as quickly as possible in the Mediterranean. He explained to the Directory in Paris that his plans were "To go to Egypt, to establish myself there and found a French Colony [which] will require several months. But, as soon as I have made England tremble for the safety of India, I shall return to Paris, and give the enemy its death-blow. There is nothing to fear in the interval. Europe is calm. Austria cannot attack. England is occupied with preparing her defenses against invasion, and Turkey will welcome the expulsion of the Mameluke."

The aims of this great expedition of 1798 were nothing if not grandiose. Napoleon was empowered by his government to occupy Egypt, exclude the English from all their possessions in the East, and seize Malta on his way through the Mediterranean. Finally, he was to have a canal cut through the Isthmus of Suez, so that France might have access to the Red Sea and, of course, to India beyond it. Napoleon's own ambitions went even further. He envisaged the day when—all the East having been conquered—he would sweep back through Turkey, smash the Ottoman Empire, and complete the encirclement of Europe. The great and revived "Roman Empire," led by France, would now encompass not only all the Mediterranean areas that had once belonged to ancient Rome but all the territories that had once fallen before Alexander the Great—as well as the extensive British possessions in India. Whatever might be said about Napoleon, he certainly never lacked ambition; even the dreams of the world conquerors of the past pale into insignificance when compared with his.

The fleet and the men were gradually assembled at Marseilles and Toulon, as well as in Genoa, Civitavecchia, and his native Corsica. Thirty thousand infantrymen were to embark on the great adventure, together with specialized companies of sappers and miners and more than a hundred fieldpieces and siege guns. The fleet would ultimately consist of thirteen ships of the line, some gunboats for bombardment, seven frigates, and about three hundred transports. Although this was a formidable armada, the number of transports was out of all proportion to the number of fighting ships designed to protect the convoy. If Nelson or any other British admiral had come upon it at sea, there can be little doubt that it would have been annihilated. What distinguished this fleet from any other that had ever crossed the Mediterranean was that it carried not only the soldiers to execute the invader's designs but a whole team of savants—some of the finest intellects in France. More than one hundred and fifty learned civilians, equipped with hundreds of books and scientific instruments, were to bring French culture to the East, as well as to discover whatever secrets lay locked in the valley of the Nile. Not even Alexander had set out with the intention of deliberately cross-fertilizing the Mediterranean basin.

The expedition finally sailed from Toulon on May 19, escaping the vigilant British only by sheer good fortune. "The Devil's children," as Nelson later remarked, "have the Devil's luck." On June 9 Malta was in sight, and Napoleon at once sent a message ashore requesting permission for his fleet to enter Grand Harbor. The Order of St. John of Jerusalem, also known as the Knights of Malta, that last surviving link with the Crusades, had long been in a state of decline, and many of the Knights were actively in league with France. Despite the fact that Malta's defenses could probably have withstood a siege for a matter of months, the island capitulated within three days. The Knights of Malta, who had guarded Europe's southern flank for two and a half centuries, were unceremoniously bundled out of their ancient home.

Napoleon had every reason thus far to be pleased with the progress of his expedition. Nelson, meanwhile, had arrived at Naples, where he heard rumors of the French landing at Malta. Pressing on furiously in pursuit, he and his ships of the line came surging down the east coast of Sicily, only to hear from the captain of a passing merchantman that Napoleon had indeed taken Malta but had already left the island for an unknown destination. Nelson, presuming quite correctly that the destination of the armada could only be Egypt, directed his course for Alexandria. The prevailing northwesterly winds served him well as he drove his ships southeastward. He reached the port on June 28, six days after leaving Sicily. There he learned to his dismay that no French ships had been sighted. To quote Admiral Mahan: "This remarkable miscarriage, happening to a man of so much energy and intuition, was due primarily to his want of small lookout ships; and secondly, to Bonaparte's using the simple, yet at sea sufficient ruse, of taking an indirect instead of a direct course to his object."

The French fleet, in fact, had taken a dog-legged route, proceeding east to Crete and thence southeast. Because of this detour, and because the heavy transports slowed the convoy's speed, Nelson, in pursuit, had unwittingly overtaken and passed his quarry. His disappointment at finding no French ships in Alexandria now caused him to

Admiral Brueys, the brave French commander, met his death in the battle with gallantry.

abandon his original, sound judgment of Napoleon's destination. On June 29, the day after arriving, he sailed northeast on the first leg of a zigzag course that would take him to a point off the coast of Asia Minor, then south of Crete, and so again to Sicily. Watchers from the Pharos of Alexandria that day had hardly seen the sails of Nelson's squadron disappear over the horizon before the sails of the immense French fleet came in sight to the northwest. Within hours Napoleon and his soldiers were at anchor.

The city he entered—putting his army ashore immediately after he heard that the English had preceded him—bore little resemblance to that proud capital in which Anthony and Cleopatra had loved and died. As Oliver Warner writes in *Nelson's Battles:*

The country which Bonaparte had entered so unceremoniously presented a picture of decay surpassing that of Malta of the Knights. . . . The flow of trade from the Far East had long ceased to pass through Egypt and the Mediterranean to the Adriatic and so into the heart of Europe. Decline, which had begun when the Portuguese discovered the sea route to India and China via the Cape of Good Hope at the end of the fif-

teenth century, had been gradual. It could perhaps have been arrested but for the greed of those who ruled the country. They inflicted so punishing a tax on the transit of goods (even after an alternative route had been shown to be practical), that no merchant would willingly face it.

Nominally subject to the Sultan of Turkey, Egypt was in fact governed by the Mamelukes, a military order who were as picturesque a survival from the time of the Crusades as the Knights of Malta. The word signified in Arabic chattel or male slave, and Mamelukes were indeed recruited as slaves from their homes in the Caucasus, their future loyalty being to their own Order [rather like the janissaries]. They did not mix with or marry Egyptians, and the real slaves of the country were the patient fellahin, the peasants, poor and exploited, on whom the whole economy depended.

Within three weeks of reaching Alexandria, Napoleon had met and defeated the Mamelukes in the celebrated Battle of the Pyramids. "Soldiers, from these pyramids forty centuries look down upon you," he reminded his men. The remark is famous, so too his victory: both were hollow. As has been proved so often in the past, in the conduct of war in the countries surrounding the Mediterranean it is essential to have command of the sea.

Nelson, back in Sicily, realized soon enough that his first surmise had been correct after all, and that Napoleon must surely be in Egypt now. He kept his fleet for a few days in the famous old harbor of Syracuse. Just before weighing anchor, he wrote to the British minister in Naples, Sir William Hamilton: "Thanks to your exertions, we have victualled and watered; and surely, watering at the Fountain of Arethusa, we must have victory. We shall sail with the first breeze, and be assured that I will return either crowned with laurel, or covered with cypress."

On August 1 the English fleet was once more off Alexandria. The harbor was full of French transports, but curiously enough, there were no large warships to be seen. The French admiral,

Brueys, had mistrusted the entrance to the port and had sailed fifteen miles farther down the coast to drop anchor in Abukir Bay. This was an immense, sand-rimmed bay, stretching some eighteen miles from Abukir Point in the west to the Rosetta Mouth of the Nile in the east. The French ships of the line were anchored in a long, slightly curved line at the western end of the bay, in the lee of Abukir Island, which lies just off the point. In addition, four frigates were anchored in an irregularly spaced line, roughly parallel to the bigger ships and between the latter and the shore. Admiral Brueys no doubt thought that he had made his disposition very skillfully, but he had, in fact, been somewhat negligent. The intervals between his ships were too great— about 160 yards on the average; the ships, moreover, were anchored only by the bows, and consequently swung with the wind. As it turned out, when Nelson arrived upon the scene the wind was from the north-northwest, and the French ships were lined up in such a way—the bowsprit of each pointing toward the stern of the next across a broad expanse of open water—as to provide an audacious adversary with significant tactical advantages. Perhaps Brueys's somewhat casual placement of his fleet had been occasioned by the same overconfidence that had made Napoleon write only two days before: "All the conduct of the English indicates that they are inferior in number, and content themselves with blockading Malta and intercepting its supplies."

At about two o'clock on the afternoon of August 1, 1798, the English sighted the French fleet snug in its haven at Abukir Bay. This was the moment for which Nelson had been waiting, and he at once steered to close the distance between the ships. Brueys, for his part, could not believe that the English would attack that day, for the French practice would have been to make a careful reconnaissance, decide on a plan of action, and wait for daylight. This was not Nelson's way, for he reckoned that he and his "Band of Brothers" would have ample time to survey the French dispositions, and prepare their plan of action, even as they drove in to attack. During the long chase around the eastern Mediterranean Nelson had been in such a fever of anxiety that he had scarcely slept or taken any food other than a quick snack. Now, seeing the whole object of his ambition lying placidly awaiting him—and aware that it would be several hours before his ships would be rounding the point to commence action—he ordered dinner to be formally served.

Shortly after six o'clock in the evening the action began. Captain Foley in the *Goliath,* the leading English ship, rounded into the bay and approached the French line. Foley's trained eye quickly observed that through the failure to moor them both fore and aft, the ships had swung to the wind. This enabled him to steer between the little island and the lead French ship, to round the latter's bow, and to take up a position on the landward side of the French line—a maneuver that would have been impossible if Brueys had made his dispositions correctly. The next four ships also passed to the landward side of the French—one, at least, boldly piercing their line between the lead ship and the ship immediately astern. The French captains were so taken aback by this unexpected move that many precious minutes passed before they could get their portside guns unencumbered and return the British fire. Nelson, in the *Vanguard,* came up

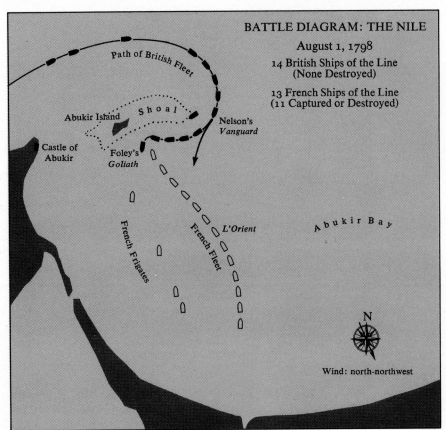

OVERLEAF: *The Battle of the Nile begins as the* Goliath, *in middle distance, rounds the head of the French column—to the intense anticipation of the Arabs at lower left, who enjoy perfect seats to watch the unfolding drama. As the diagram above shows, four British ships followed the* Goliath's *lead; then, as night fell, Nelson led the attack from the sea. The anchored French ships were caught in a deadly cross fire. By morning the scene overleaf was one of desolation: two ships of the line (right) and two frigates (left) had fled, but all the rest of the French vessels were either captured or destroyed.*

Led below with a wound he feared was mortal, Nelson (right) told a surgeon, "I will wait my turn with my brave fellows." The brave fellow at left is about to have his leg cut off without anesthesia.

just as night was falling and launched an attack from the seaward side, shortly to be followed by his next two ships. As a result, the ships in the French van found themselves engaged on both sides.

Hood, captain of the *Zealous,* in his account of the action against the French *Le Guerrier,* gives an idea of what must have been happening all up and down the line, as more and more English ships sailed up and engaged their opponents:

I commenced such a well-directed fire into her bow within pistol shot a little after six that her fore-mast went by the board in about seven minutes, just as the sun was closing the horizon; on which the whole squadron gave three cheers, it happening before the next ship astern of me had fired a shot and only the *Goliath* and *Zealous* engaged. And in ten minutes more her main and mizzen masts went; at this time also went the main mast of the second ship, engaged closely by the *Goliath* and *Audacious,* but I could not get *Le Guerrier*'s commander to strike for three hours, though I hailed him twenty times, and seeing he was totally cut up and only firing a stern gun now and then at the *Goliath* and *Audacious.*

At last being tired of firing and killing people in that way, I sent my boat on board her, and the lieutenant was allowed . . . to hoist a light and haul it down to show his submission.

The battle raged throughout the night. Nelson, who had come prepared for a night action, had given orders for his ships to show a horizontal group of lanterns so that the English could easily recognize one another. The French admiral, however, never having expected an engagement after dark, had made no such preparations. He seems to have had little knowledge of what exactly was happening, as the English slowly and methodically moved past his ships, often on both sides of them, destroying them with their concentrated fire. Brueys himself, though wounded in the head and in one hand, continued to direct the fire from his flagship *L'Orient* until a cannon ball tore off his left thigh, nearly cutting him in two. Meanwhile, a fire began to spread aboard the doomed flagship, and many of the crew started jumping into the sea to save their lives. *L'Orient*'s captain, Casabianca, whose son had been wounded, is said to have refused to desert the ship without him—an incident that gave rise to Mrs. Hemans's popular poem *Casabianca,* which begins "The boy stood on the burning deck." An English midshipman, John

Lee, who wrote his recollections of the action many years later, recorded: "The son of Casabianca had lost a leg, and was below with the surgeon, but the father could not be prevailed upon to quit the ship even to save his own life, preferring to die beside his son rather than leave him wounded, and a prey to flames."

Soon after ten o'clock the fire reached the French flagship's main magazine, and *L'Orient* exploded with a shattering crash that was heard as far away as Alexandria. The noise was so devastating that, as if by common consent, all ships stopped firing; for a brief period the action came to a halt. When the battle recommenced, it was clear that it was now no more than a tidying-up action. The French fleet, to all intents and purposes, had ceased to exist.

By daylight on August 2 *L'Orient* and one frigate were sunk, and no fewer than nine French ships of the line were either out of action or already captured or both. One other ship was run aground and set afire on her captain's orders. Only the last two ships of the French line managed to escape—together with two frigates. For the French, the affair had been a catastrophe.

Many years later, when Napoleon was a prisoner aboard the *Bellerophon,* he remarked to her captain: "In all my plans I have always been thwarted by the British fleet"; later still, while sailing for his ultimate island-prison of St. Helena, he had a life of Nelson read to him by his secretary. He clearly recognized that this was the man who had done more than any other to thwart his ambitions.

The Battle of the Nile was, in a sense, more important even than Trafalgar. It was Napoleon's first major reverse, and it put new heart into the whole of Europe. In a way it resembled Alamein in the Second World War. It showed that the apparently insuperable conquerors were as subject to defeat as any other mortals.

"My Lord," Nelson wrote to the

The battle's most awesome moment came when fires in the huge French flagship L'Orient *reached her magazines and she blew up.*

Earl of St. Vincent, "Almighty God has blessed His Majesty's Arms in the late Battle, by a great victory over the Fleet of the enemy, who I attacked at sunset on the 1st. of August, off the mouth of the Nile. The enemy were moored in a strong line of Battle for defending the entrance of the Bay (of Shoals) flanked by numerous gunboats, four frigates, and a battery of guns and mortars on an Island in their van: but nothing could withstand the Squadron your Lordship did me the honour to place under my command. Their high state of discipline is well known to you, and with the judgement of the captains, together with their valour, and that of the officers and men of every description, it was absolutely irresistible."

The news of the victory swept through Europe like a forest fire. Its effect, in an age when emotions were less restrained than now, was almost to deprive people of their senses. Sir William Hamilton's wife, Emma (soon to become deeply involved with Nelson), fell to the ground so overcome that, as Nelson wrote some days later, she "is not yet properly recovered from severe bruises." Even back in London within the austere walls of the Admiralty, Lord Spencer, on hearing the news, dropped to the floor in a dead faint. Politically, the principal result of the Battle of the Nile was to bring into being the Second Coalition against revolutionary France. Nearly all that Napoleon had gained in Italy

was swept away in one brief campaign, while Turkey now came into the war on the side of the Allies. Its greatest significance, however, was that although the war against France would yet drag on for many years, the English had now secured the domination of the Mediterranean. It was something that, while it was often challenged and sometimes imperiled, they never lost—until they vacated it of their own accord in the second half of the twentieth century.

Ernle Bradford is a British writer and broadcaster on sailing, history, and antiques. This article is excerpted from his Mediterranean: Portrait of a Sea, *to be published by Harcourt, Brace and World.*

THE COSMIC PRISON

THE SENATOR:
"We are masters of the universe. We can go anywhere we choose."

THE PHILOSOPHER:
"To speak of man as mastering the cosmos is about the equivalent of installing a grasshopper as Secretary General of the United Nations."

"A name is a prison, God is free," once observed the Greek poet Nikos Kazantzakis. He meant, I think, that valuable though language is to man, it is by very necessity limiting, and creates for man an invisible prison. Language implies boundaries. A word spoken creates a dog, a rabbit, a man. It fixes their nature before our eyes; henceforth their shapes are, in a sense, our own creation. They are no longer part of the unnamed shifting architecture of the universe. They have been transfixed as if by sorcery, frozen into a concept, a word. Powerful though the spell of human language has proved itself to be, it has laid boundaries upon the cosmos.

No matter how far-ranging some of the mental probes that man has philosophically devised, by his own created nature he is forced to hold the specious and emerging present and transform it into words. The words are startling in their immediate effectiveness, but at the same time, they are always finally imprisoning because man has constituted himself a prison keeper. He does so out of no conscious intention, but because for immediate purposes he has created an unnatural world of his own, which he calls the cultural world, and in which he feels at home. It defines his needs and allows him to lay a small immobilizing spell upon the nearer portions of his universe. Nevertheless it transforms that universe into a cosmic prison house that is no sooner mapped out than man feels its inadequacy and his own.

Scarcely had the moon flight been achieved before one U.S. Senator boldly announced: "We are the masters of the universe. We can go anywhere we choose." This statement was widely and editorially acclaimed. It is a striking example of the comfort of words, also of the covert substitutions and mental projections to which they are subject. The cosmic prison is not made less so by a successful journey of some two hundred and forty thousand miles in a cramped and primitive vehicle.

To escape the cosmic prison man is

poorly equipped. He has to drag portions of his environment with him, and his life span is that of a May fly in terms of the distances he seeks to penetrate. There is no possible way to master such a universe by flight alone. Indeed, such a dream is a dangerous illusion.

This may seem a heretical statement, but its truth is self-evident if we seriously try to comprehend the nature of time and space, which I, as a child, had grasped by intuitive perception when held up to view Halley's comet, the fiery messenger that had flared across the zenith in the spring of 1910, startling viewers innocent of science. "Seventy-five years," my father had whispered in my ear, "seventy-five years and it will be racing homeward. Perhaps you will live to see it again. Try to remember."

And so I remembered. I had gained a faint glimpse of the size of our prison house. Somewhere out there beyond a billion miles in space an entity known as a comet had rounded on its track in the black darkness of the void. It was surging homeward toward the sun because it was an eccentric satellite of this solar system. If I lived to see it, it would be but barely, and with the dimmed eyes of age. Yet it, too, in its long traverse, was but a flitting May fly in terms of the universe the night sky revealed.

So relative is the universe we inhabit that as we gaze upon the outer galaxies available to the reach of our telescopes, we are placed in about the position of a single white blood cell in our bodies, if it were intelligently capable of seeking to understand the nature of its own universe, the body it inhabits.

The cell would encounter rivers ramifying into miles of distance seemingly leading nowhere. It would pass through gigantic structures whose meaning it could never grasp—the brain, for example. It could never know there was an outside, a vast being on a scale it could not conceive of and of which it formed an infinitesimal part. It would know only the pouring tumult of the creation it inhabited, but of the nature

of that great beast, or even indeed that it was a beast, it could have no conception whatever. It might examine the liquid in which it floated and decide, as in the case of the fall of Lucretius's atoms, that the pouring of obscure torrents had created its world.

It might discover that creatures other than itself swam in the torrent. But that its universe was alive, had been born and was destined to perish, its own ephemeral existence would never allow it to perceive. It would never know the sun; it would explore only through dim tactile sensations and react to chemical stimuli that were borne to it along the mysterious conduits of the arteries and veins. Its universe would be centered upon a great arborescent tree of spouting blood. This, at best, generations of white cells, by enormous labor and continuity, might succeed in charting.

They could never, by any conceivable stretch of the imagination, be aware that their so-called universe was in actuality the prowling body of a cat or the more time-enduring body of a philosopher, himself engaged upon the same quest in a more gigantic world and perhaps deceived proportionately by greater vistas. What if, for example, the far galaxies that man observes make up, across void spaces of which even we are atomically composed, some kind of enormous creature or cosmic snowflake whose exterior we will never see? We will know more than the phagocyte in our bodies, but no more than that limited creature can we climb out of our universe, or successfully enhance our size or longevity sufficiently to thrust our heads through the confines of the universe that terminates our vision.

Some further "outside" will hover elusively in our thought, but upon its nature, or even its reality, we can do no more than speculate. The phagocyte might observe the salty turbulence of an eternal river system, Lucretius the fall of atoms creating momentary living shapes. We suspiciously sense, in the concept of the expanding universe

By LOREN EISELEY

derived from the primordial atom, some kind of oscillating universal heart. At the instant of its contraction we will vanish. It is not given us to know, nor can our science recapture, the state beyond the monobloc, nor whether we exist in the diastole of some inconceivable being. We know only a little more extended reality than does the hypothetical creature below us. Above us may lie realism it is beyond our power to grasp.

This, then, is the secret nature of the universe over which the ebullient senator so recklessly proclaimed our absolute mastery. Time in that universe is in excess of ten billion years. It recedes backward into a narrowing funnel where, at some inconceivable point of concentration, the monobloc, or "primeval atom," containing all the matter that composes the galaxies exploded in the one gigantic instant of creation.

Along with that explosion, space itself is rushing outward. Stars and the great island galaxies in which they cluster are more numerous than the blades of grass upon a plain. To speak of man as "mastering" such a cosmos is about the equivalent of installing a grasshopper as Secretary General of the United Nations. Worse, in fact, for no matter what system of propulsion man may invent in the future, the galaxies on the outer rim of visibility are fleeing faster than he can approach them. Moreover, the light he is receiving from them left its source in the early history of the planet Earth. There is no possible way of even establishing their present existence. As the British astronomer Bernard Lovell has so appropriately remarked, "At the limit of present-day observations our information is a few billion years out of date."

It has been estimated that the time required to reach the nearest star to our own, four light-years away, would be, at the present speed of our spaceships, the equivalent of more than the whole of written history; indeed one hundred thousand years would be a closer estimate—a time as long, perhaps, as the whole existence of Homo sapiens upon earth. And the return, needless to state, would consume just as long a period.

Even if our present rocket speeds were stepped up by a factor of a hundred, human generations would pass on the voyage. An unmanned probe into the nearer galactic realms would be gone so long that its intended mission, and the country that sent it forth, might both have vanished into the mists of history before its messages could begin to be received. All this, be it noted, does not begin to involve us in those intergalactic distances across which a radio message from a spaceship might take thousands of years to be received and a wait of more thousands before a reply would filter back.

Two years ago I chanced to wander with a group of visiting scholars into a small planetarium in a nearby city. In the dark in a remote back seat, I grew tired and fell asleep while a lecture was progressing. My eyes had closed upon a present-day starry night as represented in the northern latitudes. After what seemed in my uneasy slumber the passage of a long period of time, I started awake in the dark, my eyes fixed in amazement upon the star vault overhead. All was quiet in the neighboring high-backed seats. I could see no one. Suddenly I seemed adrift under a vast and unfamiliar sky. Constellations with which I was familiar had shifted, grown minute, or vanished. I rubbed my eyes. This was not the same universe in which I had fallen asleep. A queer sense of panic struck me; it was as though I had been transported out of time.

Only after some attempt to orient myself by a diminished polestar did the answer come to me by murmurs from without. I was not the last man on the planet, far in the dying future. My companions had arisen and left, while the lecturer had terminated his address by setting the planetarium lights forward to show the conformation of the heavens as they might exist in the remote future of the expanding universe. Distances had lengthened. All was poised, chill, and alone.

I sat for a moment, experiencing the sensation all the more intensely because of the slumber that had left me feeling as though ages had elapsed. The sky gave little sign of movement. It seemed to be drifting in a slow, indeterminate swirl, as though the forces of expansion were equaled at last by some monstrous tug of gravity at the heart of things. In this remote night-sky of the far future I felt myself waiting for the inevitable, the great drama and surrender of the inward fall, the heart contraction of the cosmos.

I was still sitting when, like the slightest leaf movement on a flooding stream, I saw the first faint galaxy of a billion suns race like silverfish across the night and vanish. It was enough: the fall was equal to the flash of creation. I had sensed it waiting there under the star vault of the planetarium. Now it was cascading like a torrent through the ages in my head. I had experienced, by chance, the farthest reach of the star prison. I had also lived to see the beginning descent into the maelstrom.

There are other confinements, however, than that imposed by the enormous distances of the cosmos. One could almost list them. There is, for example, the prison of smells. I happen to know a big black hunting poodle named Beau. Beau loves to go for walks in the woods, and at such times as I visit his owners the task of seeing Beau safely through his morning adventures is happily turned over to me.

Beau has eyes, of course, and I do not doubt that he uses them when he greets his human friends by proffering a little gift such as his food dish. After this formality, which dates from his puppyhood, has been completed, Beau reverts to the world of snuffles. As a long-time and trusted friend, I have frequently tried to get Beau to thrust his head out of the world of smells and actually to see the universe. I have led him before the mirror in my bedroom and tried to persuade him to see himself, his own visible identity. The results, it turns out, are totally unsatisfactory, if not ludicrous. Beau peers out from his black ringlets as suspiciously as an ape hiding in a bush. He immediately drops his head and pretends to examine the floor. It is evident he detests this apparition and has no intention of being cajoled into some dangerous, undoggy wisdom by my voice.

He promptly brings his collar and makes appropriate throaty conversation. To appease his wounded feelings, I set out for a walk in the woods. It is necessary to do this with a long chain, and a very tight grasp upon it. Beau is a big, powerful animal, and ringlets or no, he has come from an active and carnivorous past. Once in the woods all this past suddenly emerges. One is dragged willy-nilly through leaf, thorn, and thicket on intangible trails that Beau's swinging muzzle senses upon the wind.

His deep, wet nose has entered a world denied to me—a mad world whose contours and direction change with every gust of air. I leap and bound with a chafed wrist through a smell universe I cannot even sense. Occasionally something squawks or bounds from under our feet and I am flung against trees or wrapped around by a flying chain.

On one memorable occasion, after a rain, Beau paused, sniffing suspiciously between two rocks on a hillside. Another rabbit, I groaned mentally, taking a tighter hold on the chain. Beau then began some careful digging, curving and patting the soil aside in a way I had never before witnessed. A small basin shaped by Beau's forepaws presently appeared, and up from the bottom of it welled a spring-fed pool in which Beau promptly buried his snout and lapped long and lustily of water that I am sure carried the living tastes and delicate nuances of information disseminated from an unseen watershed.

Beau had had a proper drink of tap water before we started from home,

but this drink was different. I could tell from the varied, eager slurping sounds that emanated from Beau. He was intoxicated by living water that dim primordial memories had instructed him how to secure. I looked on, interested and sympathetic, but aware that the big black animal lived in a smell prison as I, in my way, lived in a sight prison. Our universes intersected sufficiently for us to be aware, in a friendly fashion, of each other, but Beau would never admit the mirror image of himself into his mind, and try as I would, the passing breeze would never inform me of the shadowy creatures that passed unglimpsed in the forest.

There are, of course, still other prisons in the universe than those dominated by the senses of smell or sight or temperature. Some involve the length of a creature's lifetime, as in the case of five-year-old Beau, who gambols happily about his master, knowing him to be one of the everlasting immortals of his universe.

The dream that there are men elsewhere in the universe, alleviating the final prison of human loneliness, dies hard. Nevertheless, a wise remark Santayana made many years ago should discourage facile and optimistic thinking upon this very point. "An infinite number of solar systems," the philosopher meditated, "must have begun as ours began, but each of them must have deviated at one point from ours in its evolution, all the previous incidents being followed in each case by a different sequel." In voicing this view, Santayana betrays a clearer concept of the chance-filled course of genetics and its unreturning pathways than that of some astronomers. The Mendelian pathways are prisons of no return. Advances are made, but always a door swings shut behind the evolving organism. It can no longer mate with its one-time progenitors. It can only press forward along roads that increasingly will fix its irrevocable destiny.

Ours is a man-centered age. Not many months ago I was perusing a work on space when I came across this statement by a professional astronomer: "Other stars, other planets, other life, and other races of men are evolving all along, so that the net effect is changeless." Implied in this remark was an utter confidence that the evolutionary process was everywhere the same, ran through the same succession of forms, and emerged always with men at the helm of life, men presumably so close to ourselves that they might interbreed—a supposition fostered by our comic strips.

In the light of this naive concept—for such it is—let us consider just two worlds we know about, not worlds in space, but continents on our own planet. These continents exist under the same sun and are surrounded by the same waters as our own; their life bears a distant relationship to ours but has long been isolated. Man never arose in the remote regions of South America and Australia. He only reached them by migration from outside. They are laboratories of age-long evolution that tell us much about the unique quality of the human experience.

The southern continents of our earth do not maintain the intimacy of faunal exchange that marks the Holarctic land masses encircling the basin of the polar sea. Instead, they are lost in the southern latitudes of the oceans, and for long intervals their faunas have evolved in isolation. These lands have been, in truth, "other worlds."

The most isolated of these worlds is Australia. With the insignificant exception of a few late drifters from outside, this marsupial world is not merely an ancient world. It is a world in which ground life, originally represented by a few marsupial forms, has, since the Mesozoic era, evolved untroubled by invading placental mammals from without. Every possible ecological niche from forest tree to that of underground burrower has been occupied by the evolutionary radiation of a slower-brained mammal whose young are born in a far more embryonic condition than that of the true Placentalia.

This world remained unknown to Western science until the great exploratory voyages began. Somewhere in the past, life had taken another turn. Chance mutation, "total contingency" in the words of the American paleontologist William King Gregory, had led to another universe. The "world" of Australia contained no primates at all, nor any hint of their emergence. Upon that "planet" lost in the great waters they were one of an infinite number of random potentialities that had remained as unrealized as the whole group of placental mammals, of which the Primate order is a minor part.

If we now turn to South America, we encounter still another isolated evolutionary center—but one not totally unrelated to that of Eurasia. Here, so the biogeographers inform us, an attenuated land bridge, at intervals completely severed, has both stimulated local evolutionary development and at times interrupted it by migrations from North America. Our concern is with just one group of animals, the South American monkeys. They are anatomically distinct from the catarrhine forms of the Old World, and constitute an apparent parallel emergence from the prosimians of the early Tertiary.

Once more, however, despite the fact that the same basic primate stock is involved, things have gone differently. There are no great apes in the New World, no evidence of ground-dwelling experiments of any kind. Though fewer carnivores are to be found on the South American grasslands than in Africa, the rain-forest monkeys, effectively equipped with prehensile tails, still cling to their archaic pathways. One can only observe that South America's vast rivers flow through frequently flooded lowlands, and that by contrast much of Africa is high, with open savanna and parkland. The South American primates appear to be confined to areas where descent to the ground proved less in-

viting. Here ended another experiment that did not lead to man, though it began within the same order from which he sprang. Another world had gone astray from the human direction.

If, some occasionally extrapolate, man was so ubiquitous, so easy to produce, why did two great continental laboratories, Australia and South America —"worlds," indeed—fail to reproduce him? They failed, we may assume, simply because the great movements of life are irreversible, the same mutations do not occur, circumstances differ in infinite particulars, opportunities fail to be grasped, and so, what once happened is no more. The random element is always present, but it is selected on the basis of what has preceded it.

There appears to be nothing foreordained about the human emergence, nor any trend demanding man's constant reappearance, either on what we have seen to be the separate "worlds" of this world or elsewhere. There can no more be a random duplication of man than there is a random duplication of such a complex genetic phenomenon as fingerprints. The situation is not one that is comparable to a single identical cast of dice, but rather it is an endless addition of new genes building on what has previously been incorporated into a living creature through long ages. Nature gambles, but she gambles with constantly new and altering dice. It is this well-established fact that enables us to call long-range evolution irreversible.

Finally, there are even meteorological prisons. The constant circulation of moisture in our atmosphere actually played an important role in creating the first vertebrates and, indirectly, man. If early rivers had not poured from the continents into the sea, the first sea vertebrates to penetrate streams above sea level would not have evolved a rigid muscular support, the spine, to enable them to wriggle against down-rushing currents. And if man, in his

early history, had not become a tree climber in tropical rain-forests, he would never have further tilted that same spine upright or replaced the smell prison of the horizontal mammal with the stereoscopic, far-ranging "eye brain" of the higher primates. If space permitted, such final dice throws, in which leaf and grass, wave and water, are inextricably commingled with the chemistry of the body, could be multiplied. The cosmic prison is subdivided into an infinite number of unduplicable smaller prisons, the prisons of form.

We are now in a position to grasp, after an examination of the many prisons that encompass life, that the cosmic prison many men, in the excitement of the first moon landing, believed we had escaped, still extends immeasurably beyond us. The lack of any conceivable means of travel and the shortness of our individual lives both prevent the crossing of such distances. Even if we confined ourselves to unmanned space probes of far greater sophistication than those we now possess, their homing messages through the void could be expected to descend upon the ruined radio scanners of a civilization long vanished, or upon one whose aging scholars would have long since forgotten what naive dreams had been programmed into such instruments. We have detected that we exist in a prison of numbers, otherwise known as light-years. We are also locked in a body that responds to biological rather than sidereal time. That body, in turn, receives the universe through its own senses and through no others.

At every turn of thought a lock snaps shut upon us. As societal men we bow to a given frame of culture—a world view we have received from the past. Biologically each of us is unique, and the tight spiral of the DNA molecules conspires to doom us to mediocrity or grandeur. We dream vast dreams of utopias and live to learn the meaning of a Greek philosopher's judgment: "The flaw is in the vessel itself"—the flaw that defeats all governments.

By what means, then, can we seek escape from groveling in mean corners of despair? Not, certainly, by the rush to depart upon the night's black pathways, nor by attention to the swerving wind vane of the senses. We are men, and despite all our follies there have been great ones among us who have counseled us in wisdom, men who have also sought keys to our prison. Strangely, these men have never spoken of space; they have spoken, instead, as though the farthest spaces lay within the mind itself—as though we still carried a memory of some light of long ago and the way we had come. Perhaps for this reason alone we have scanned the skies and the waters with what Henry Vaughan so well labeled the "Ecclips'd Eye," that eye incapable of quite assembling the true meaning of the universe but striving to do so "with Hyeroglyphicks quite dismembered."

These are the words of a seventeenth-century mystic who has mentally dispatched inward vision through all the creatures until coming to man, who "shines a little" and whose depths he finds it impossible to plumb. Thomas Traherne, another man of that century of the Ecclips'd Eye, when religion was groping amid the revelations of science, stated well the matter of the keys to the prison.

"Infinite love," he ventured, "cannot be expressed in finite room. Yet it must be infinitely expressed in the smallest moment . . . Only so is it in both ways infinite."

Can this insight be seen to justify itself in modern evolutionary terms? I think it can.

Close to a hundred years ago the great French medical scientist Claude Bernard observed that the stability of the inside environment of complex organisms must be maintained before an outer freedom can be achieved from their immediate surroundings. What Bernard meant was profound but is simple to illustrate.

He meant that for life to obtain relative security from its fickle and dangerous outside surroundings the animal must be able to sustain stable, unchanging conditions within the body. Warm-blooded mammals and birds can continue to move about in winter; insects cannot. Warm-blooded animals such as man, with his stable body temperature, can continue to think and reason in outside temperatures that would put a frog to sleep in a muddy pond or roll a snake into a ball in a crevice. In winter latitudes many of the lower creatures are forced to sleep part of their lives away.

It took many millions of years of evolutionary effort before life was successful in defending its internal world from the intrusion of the heat or cold of the outside world of nature. Yet only so can life avoid running down like a clock in winter or perishing from exposure to the midday sun. Even the desert rattlesnake is forced to coil in the shade of a bush at midday. Of course our tolerance is limited to a few degrees of temperature when measured against the great thermometer of the stars, but this hard-won victory is what creates the ever active brain of the mammal against the retarded sluggishness of the reptile.

A steady metabolism has enabled the birds and mammals to experience life more fully and rapidly than cold-blooded creatures. One of the great feats of evolution, perhaps the greatest, has been this triumph of the interior environment over exterior nature. Inside, we might say, has fought invading outside, and inside, since the beginning of life, has by slow degrees won the battle of life. If it had not, man, frail man with his even more fragile brain, would not exist.

Unless fever or some other disorder disrupts this internal island of safety, we rarely think of it. Body controls are normally automatic, but let them once go wrong and outside destroys inside. This is the simplest expression of the war of nature—the endless conflict between the microcosm and macrocosm.

Since the first cell created a film about itself and elected to carry on the carefully insulated processes known as life, the creative spark has not been generalized. Whatever its principle may be, it hides magically within individual skins. To the day of our deaths we exist in an inner solitude that is linked to the nature of life itself. Even as we project love and affection upon others, we endure a loneliness that is the price of all individual consciousness: the price of living.

It is, though overlooked, the discontinuity beyond all others: the separation both of the living creature from the inanimate and of the individual from his kind. These are star distances. In man, moreover, consciousness looks out isolated from its own body. The body is the true cosmic prison, yet it contains, in the creative individual, a magnificent if sometimes helpless giant.

John Donne spoke for that giant in each of us. He said: "Our creatures are our thoughts, creatures that are borne Gyants . . . My thoughts reach all, comprehend all. Inexplicable mystery; I their Creator am in a close prison, in a sick bed, anywhere, and any one of my Creatures, my thoughts is with the Sunne and beyond the Sunne, overtakes the Sunne, and overgoes the Sunne in one pace, one steppe, everywhere."

This thought, expressed so poignantly by Donne, represents the final triumph of Claude Bernard's interior microcosm in its war with the macrocosm. Inside has conquered outside. The giant confined in the body's prison roams at will among the stars. More rarely and more beautifully, perhaps, the profound mind in the close prison projects infinite love in a finite room. This is a crossing beside which light years are meaningless. It is the solitary key to the prison that is man.

Loren Eiseley is chairman of the anthropology department at the University of Pennsylvania. This article is from his new book The Invisible Pyramid, *to be published by Charles Scribner's Sons.*

"Not two flutes, you scoundrels! Two piccolos! Two piccolos! Oh, what brutes!"

All his life Hector Berlioz tried to set the musical world straight and win acceptance for music that "sets in vibration the most unexplored depths of the human soul." Mostly, he frightened everyone

"Berlioz (Hector), compositeur français . . ." The bare facts of his life, compiled by an anonymous pedant for an 1858 biographical dictionary (see pages 106–107), provoke a flurry of scribbled rebuttals from Berlioz himself. His pen fairly spatters with indignation as he emends the article submitted to him by the publishers of the *Dictionnaire Universel des Contemporaines.* And he has every right to be annoyed, for brief as it is, the article manages to slip in most of the slanders and half-truths that were then (and are still) in circulation as the standard Berlioz clichés.

From the very beginning of his career Berlioz had tried, unsuccessfully, to defend himself against these tedious misconceptions: no, he was not a composer of program music dependent on literary explanations; no, he was not a hysteric specializing in bizarre effects; and no, he was not obsessed with grandiose spectacles and overblown orchestrations. Once, when his friend Heinrich Heine described him as "a colossal nightingale or gigantic lark, a creature

Battle-scarred and melancholy, Berlioz sat for the photograph opposite in 1863, the year Les Troyens à Carthage *premièred in Paris.*

of the antediluvian world," Berlioz had explained, very patiently, that only a handful of his works—notably the *Requiem*—called for "colossal" effects; the rest were "conceived on an ordinary scale and require no exceptional means of execution."

The characteristic Berlioz sound, in fact, is wiry and almost austere when compared with the heavy, emollient orchestrations favored by most composers of the romantic school. Yet obviously there was something about his music that frightened his contemporaries in some indefinable way; he made them uneasy, just as Beethoven's last quartets made them uneasy, by going against the prevailing grain. The intensity with which he entered into everything—the same furious intensity we see at work on the proof sheets—was disconcerting to a public that regarded music as an entertainment, as a pleasantly melodious way of passing an evening at the opera or the concert hall, where one might occasionally be swept off one's feet by a Liszt, a Pasta, or a Paganini.

Paris certainly had never known a composer so deeply committed to the idea of music as an art that "sets in vibration the most unexplored depths

of the human soul." Like Beethoven, who had described himself as a Bacchus pressing out the grapes that make men spiritually drunken, Berlioz wanted to awaken a whole world of feelings and sensations that had not even existed before. On such a serious quest there was no time to be wasted on trivia (which is one of the reasons he had no use for Rossini). His elective affinities were with other men of great themes and passions: Goethe, Byron, Shakespeare, Virgil—*Faust, Romeo,* the *Aeneid.* Rising on the romantic literary landscape, his sun illuminated only the highest peaks of the range.

"The dominant qualities of my music are passionate expression, inner fire, rhythmic drive and the element of surprise," he writes in his *Memoirs,* and it is precisely these qualities that make his works so difficult to perform and hard to understand. "To render them properly the performers, and especially the conductor, ought to feel as I do. They require a combination of extreme precision and irresistible verve, a regulated vehemence, a dreamy tenderness and an almost morbid melancholy, without which the principal features of my music are either distorted or completely effaced. It is,

By FREDERIC V. GRUNFELD

therefore, as a rule, exceedingly painful to me to hear my compositions conducted by anyone but myself."

No one else on the scene had Berlioz's grasp of the orchestra as a great socio-musical instrument, as a vast organ of sound-producing enterprise. He was the first great conductor, and also the first great orchestrator, because, as Liszt observed, he possessed "the most powerful musical brain in France." Unlike his colleagues, who were accustomed to working out a composition on the piano before arranging it for orchestra, Berlioz always conceived his music orchestrally from the ground up. By the same token, it is impossible to give a clear idea of his scores by playing them on a piano. When he was a student, prize juries at the Conservatoire judged orchestral entries on the basis of piano auditions, and Berlioz forfeited several important awards because his efforts were either pronounced unplayable or mutilated in performance. "For instrumental composers," he said ruefully, "the piano is a veritable guillotine that severs the head of nobleman and churl with the same impartial indifference."

It was largely a matter of chance that he did not become a composer-pianist like everybody else. As luck would have it, there was no piano in the house when he began studying music as a boy; instead he learned to play "those three majestic incomparable instruments, the flageolet [first cousin to a recorder], the flute and the guitar." Years later, he realized that this circumstance had shaped his whole *Weltanschauung*. "When I consider the appalling platitudes to which the piano has given birth," he wrote, "I give grateful thanks to the good fortune that forced me to compose freely and in silence, and delivered me from the tyranny of the fingers, so dangerous to thought . . ."

Everything he wrote is conditioned by the fact that he was not subject to piano habits. The way he spaces out his orchestral chords and shapes his melodic phrases reveals a fresh, flexible mind that has been trained in the school of the guitar rather than the boxed-in formulas of keyboard harmony. The famous *idée fixe* melody of the *Symphonie Fantastique,* for example, is the kind of tune that might have slipped out as he was noodling on the flageolet, and its fragile harmonic setting is something that would occur only to a guitarist. Actually, neither flute nor guitar interested him as virtuoso instruments; they were only steppingstones to a career as a virtuoso with the orchestra. His bravura études are all studies in tone color—like the extraordinary duet in the "Scene in the Fields" of the *Fantastique,* where a solo oboe and a solo English horn call to each other like two shepherds across a valley. Anyone else would have written it for two oboes. But Berlioz was extremely fussy about such details at a time when the musical establishment was still largely indifferent to them. That also accounts for the amazing scenes he used to make at the Paris Opéra in his student days, when he took it upon himself to serve as a one-man watchdog committee for Weber and Gluck. The playwright Ernest Legouvé remembered afterward how he caught his first glimpse of Berlioz at a performance of Weber's *Der Freischütz* in 1832. "Suddenly, in the middle of the ritornello of Caspar's aria, one of my neighbors leaps to his feet, leans over toward the orchestra and shouts in a thundering voice:

"'Not two flutes, you scoundrels! Two piccolos! Two piccolos! Oh, what brutes!'"

It was Berlioz in fine fettle—the only man in Paris who knew or cared that they had substituted flutes for piccolos. Legouvé, who became a close friend, has left us a memorable description of how he looked at that moment: "a young man quivering with rage, his hands clenched, eyes flashing and an amazing head of hair, but what a head of hair! It was like an immense umbrella of hair, overhanging and waving about the beak of a bird of prey. It was comic and diabolical at the same time."

Berlioz always responded physically and emphatically to any musical stimulus, pleasant or unpleasant; he was the perfect example of what Virgil Thomson calls the *audito-visceral* type, "persons whose reactions to sound and to the memory of it are organic rather than visual or muscular." Like Don Juan's lust for women, Berlioz's passion for sound was constant and unquenchable. At twenty-one, after hearing his fledgling mass performed at Saint-Roch, he reported: "My breast blew out like the orchestra, the throbbings of my heart followed the blows of the kettle-drummer's stick . . . I floated on this agitated sea; I swallowed these waves of sinister vibrations."

On the podium, in front of an orchestra, he sometimes experienced a sort of rapture of the deeps—"a peal of bells in my heart, a mill-wheel in my head, my knees knocking against each other . . ." That was when he was most truly in his element, but the chance did not come nearly often enough, for Paris, that "musicians' inferno," had no real use for a virtuoso conductor. The doors of the opera houses and orchestral societies, all run by his rivals, remained resolutely closed to him for many years. The upshot was that he had to pay for the privilege of conducting his own music, often hiring the hall, singers, and instrumentalists out of his own pocket. Musically there was one advantage to being the perpetual outsider: he could disregard the practical limits of symphony orchestras as they then existed and compose experimentally on any scale he pleased. Financially, however, the results were usually disastrous. "Our art, as we understand it, is an art of millionaires," he wrote bitterly to Liszt.

There were times he almost envied Liszt his easy access to the public ear. Unable to make money either on the concert platform or as a composer of operatic hits, à la Meyerbeer, Berlioz had to fall back on writing articles for a living—a fate worse than Sisyphus's (I can vouch for it). Though at first it gave him a certain influence in the community, the chore of turning out his regular feature on music for the *Journal des Débats* gradually became a form of "penal servitude" that poisoned his existence. The issue is complicated by the fact that he did it brilliantly. For thirty years, rain or shine, he had significant things to say about the state of music in Paris, "that barbarous city," and about concert life elsewhere in Europe. Some of these essays were later incorporated into his *Memoirs*—one of the great classics of French autobiography—and into collections like *Les Soirées de l'Orchestre* and *Les Grotesques de la Musique*. No other critical essays, not even those by Bernard Shaw, can hold a candle to them; or better said, just as Berlioz's collected letters, in Flaubert's estimation, "surpass the correspondence of Balzac by 36,000 arms' lengths," so his essays surpass all other writing on music by 72,000 arms' lengths. That may not be saying very much, for music criticism is admittedly the dreariest branch of literature, but Berlioz's belongs in a totally different category: it is witty, informative, profound, poetic, generous, and the only music criticism in history that is exciting to read. The trouble was that it cost him, a musician, a terrible price to make it so:

Let them give me scores to write, orchestras to conduct, rehearsals to direct: let me stand eight or ten hours at a time, baton in hand, training choirs without accompaniment and singing the missing parts myself, beating time till I spit blood and till my arm is paralyzed by cramp; let me carry desks, double basses, harps, remove steps, nail planks like a commissionaire or a carpenter, and then by way of rest, let me correct proofs or copies at night. All this I have done and will do. It is part of my life as a musician ... But everlastingly to write newspaper articles for one's bread! ... This is the lowest depth of degradation! Better to be finance minister of a republic!

Berlioz's father, Dr. Louis-Joseph Berlioz, had planned a more prosperous

TEXT CONTINUED ON PAGE 108

Berlioz in Action

A flamboyant manner, and flamboyant music, made Berlioz an apt subject for satirists. Cham's sketch appeared in 1863, soon after the première of *Les Troyens*. Grandville drew him conducting, among other things, a cannon, with a deafened and dazed audience looking on; while Doré captured perfectly the bushy hair and extravagant gestures.

"A concert with grapeshot and Berlioz," by Grandville, 1846.

"Troy relieved, or If only they had had the score . . .," by Cham.

Berlioz conducting the Société Philharmonique, 1850, after a drawing by Gustave Doré

The Facts of Life

Hector Berlioz, the romantic composer, was all business when the subject matter dealt with the facts of his life. A biographical profile published in 1858 (shown in facsimile below, with a translation at right above) was sent to him for correction—and correct he did. Underlining the offending passages with a bold hand, scattering his comments in the margins of the neatly impersonal pages (a translation appears at right below), Berlioz acidly attacked the anonymous author, and couldn't resist aiming a few barbs at his enemies in the musical establishment. The all but unknown document was discovered by our author while leafing through an obscure 1911 publication for autograph collectors.

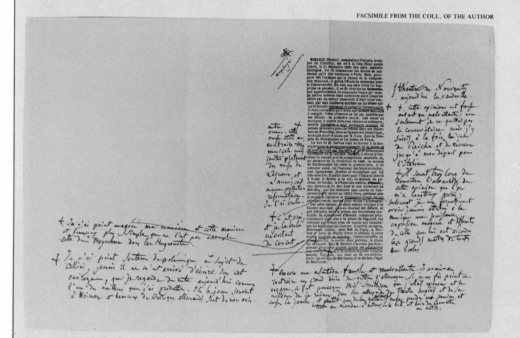

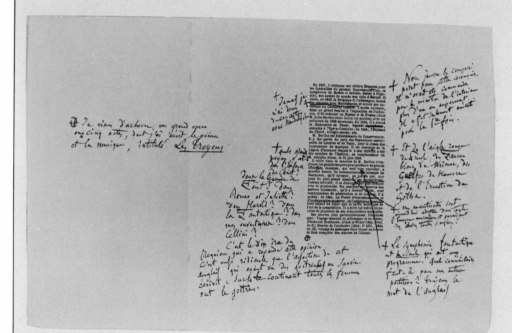

BERLIOZ (Hector), French composer, member of the Institute, was born at La Côte-Saint-André (Isère) on December 11, 1803. His father, a distinguished physician, had him undertake a program of medical studies, which he went to Paris to continue. Since childhood, however, he had been pursued by the demon of musical composition, and he left the School of Medicine for the Conservatoire. In vain did his irate father cut off his allowance; Berlioz became a chorister at the Gymnasium (1), with a salary of fifty francs a month. At that time his already ardent nature was overheated almost to a point of delirium by a passionate love affair. He was sustained, too, by supreme self-assurance, which soon led him to despise the Conservatoire and leave it (2). He was convinced that he had a musical mission to fulfill. This belief was not borne out by his initial efforts: his first work, a mass set to music for four voices with choirs and an orchestra, seemed devoid of all musical feeling (3). His musical thought revealed itself more clearly in his *Waverly Overture,* his *Symphonie Fantastique,* arranged for piano by Liszt, in *La Tempête* of Shakespeare and scenes from Faust.

Berlioz's aim was to endow music with all the expressive power of poetry and to

Berlioz's Comments

(1) The Théâtre des Nouveautés, now the Vaudeville.

(2) This assertion is false as well as malicious; not only did I not leave the Conservatoire, but I took courses there under Reicha and Lesueur at the same time until my departure for Italy.

(3) Another error: this mass was, on the contrary, very musical, but flatly imitative of Lesueur's masses, and did not display the slightest pretensions to innovation. I burned it.

(4) It would take too long to demonstrate the absurdity of this notion, which people have been pinning on me for years; I simply deny categorically that I have ever attributed to music an exaggerated expressive power different from that granted it by the great masters of all schools.

depict everything by means of effects (**4**). He was not concerned about melody in the least. In 1828, he won the Institute's second prize for musical composition, and while the 1830 revolution was raging, his cantata *Sardanapale* earned him first prize. In honor of the heroes of the July revolution he also had a *Symphonie Funèbre et Triomphale* performed that was greatly admired. He then departed for Italy, and in Rome wrote *Le Retour à la Vie; La Ballade du Pêcheur,* from Goethe's work; *Le Choeur des Ombres,* from *Hamlet;* an overture for *King Lear* and another for *Rob Roy,* which was performed without success at the Conservatoire (**5**). In 1832 he returned to Paris, having little regard for Italian music and disdaining to use his prerogatives (**6**) as an award-winner to visit Germany.

At this time he began writing criticism for *La Gazette Musicale* and then for the *Journal des Débats,* and was consequently able to defend his musical innovations in the press. His *Symphonie d'Harold,* composed principally for alto at the request of Paganini, was performed by Urhan with a success that encouraged the composer to further audacities. He wrote an opera, *Benvenuto Cellini,* for which de Vigny, A. Barbier, and Léon de Wailly furnished the libretto. Once again he had pushed his manner too far (**7**); the management turned against him, the public was forewarned, and the opera was a shattering failure. Berlioz, however, would not accept the general verdict and carried on a lively controversy with his adversaries (**8**), as a consequence of which he fell ill. Paganini, who was one of his admirers, sent him 20,000 francs and declared him the equal of Beethoven.

In 1837, he composed his famous *Requiem* for the funeral of General Damrémont (**9**). Then his *Roméo et Juliette* symphony, dedicated to Paganini, achieved as great a success as *Harold.* In 1843, he visited Belgium and Germany, gave some concerts with Mendelssohn (**10**), and wrote his *Carnaval Romain* overture. The following year, at a gala festival at the industrial exposition, he performed a *Hymne à la France* (for which Jules Barbier provided the words), with an orchestra of 1,000 musicians. In 1846, he produced *La Damnation de Faust,* a symphonic legend, performed at the Opéra Comique; in 1854, *L'Enfance du Christ,* a sacred trilogy; etc.

Berlioz is librarian of the Conservatoire. He was on the jury for musical instruments at the universal expositions in both London and Paris. He has been a chevalier of the Legion of Honor since May 5, 1839 (**11**). He was elected a member of the Institute, to fill the place of Adolphe Adam, on June 21, 1856.

It is Berlioz's way to employ grandiose means to produce grandiose effects (**12**). His music, which tries to express too much, often requires written commentary (**13**). Beethoven's example, which he invokes, does not, for most people, justify his eccentricities (**14**). As a writer he has earned distinction for his lively and impassioned criticism. His analyses of the works of the German masters, whom he frequently imitates, are notable for their insight and soundness. In 1844 he published a *Traité d'instrumentation et d'orchestration moderne,* in which musical aesthetics occupy as prominent a place as the technical side of the art of composition. He himself has written the words accompanying several of his musical compositions.

His literary works include: *Voyage musicale en Allemagne et en Italie; Études sur Beethoven, Glück et Weber* (1845, 2 vol, 8 mo); *Soirées de l'orchestre* (1853; 2nd ed. 1854, 18 mo), a volume of miscellanies that contains a complete list of the author's works (**15**).

(**5**) This is true, and I burned it when I left the concert hall.

(**6**) Another false and malicious assertion. On the contrary, I had a great desire to visit Germany. I did not make this journey because Miss Smithson, whom I was going to marry, had the misfortune of going bankrupt with her Théâtre Anglais enterprise and of breaking her leg, and I would have preferred to lose my pension and everything else in the world rather than leave her at that moment. The author of this article is clearly a long way from knowing my motives.

(**7**) I didn't push my manner too far at all, and that manner is much simpler than, for example, that of Meyerbeer in Les Huguenots.

(**8**) I did not carry on any controversy whatever on the subject of Cellini, and I have never written about this work, which, moreover, I regard today as one of the best I have produced. It is often staged in Weimar, and many German critics share my opinion.

(**9**) No, I did not compose it for that ceremony. It had been commissioned more than a year earlier by the Minister of the Interior. It was simply performed on that occasion for the first time.

(**10**) I have never given a concert with Mendelssohn.

(**11**) And of the order of the Red Eagle of Prussia, of the White Falcon of Weimar, of the Guelfs of Hannover, and of the ernestine of Gotha.

(**12**) What grandiose means are employed in L'Enfance du Christ? In the legend of Faust? In Romeo and Juliet? In Harold? In the Fantastique? In my overtures? In Cellini? It is the Dies irae of the Requiem that has given rise to this notion. It is as ridiculous as the assumption of that Englishman who, having seen some goitrous women in Savoy, wrote: on the Continent, all women have goiters.

(**13**) The Symphonie Fantastique is *the only one* that has a program. What commentaries do my other scores require? As always, the joke about the Englishman.

(**14**) My eccentricities have now been adopted by all of musical Europe and seem to consist of very simple things.

(**15**) I have just finished a grand opera in five acts, for which I wrote the libretto and the music, entitled *Les Troyens.*

TEXT CONTINUED FROM PAGE 105

and predictable career for him; he was to have succeeded to the doctor's flourishing practice as a small-town physician in La Côte-Saint-André, which lies between Grenoble and Lyon in that beautiful region of France where the western Alps begin. Both parents came from well-to-do families, and Dr. Berlioz, a freethinker who distrusted the local schools, chose to educate the boy himself. In the *Memoirs* he is gratefully remembered as "a patient, unwearied, careful, clever teacher of languages, literature, history and geography." It was from him that Berlioz had his first flute lessons and acquired a taste for Latin literature. The epic poetry of Virgil "first kindled my smouldering imagination," he says, and he recalls how his voice shook and his heart throbbed while translating the fourth book of the *Aeneid* with his father. When he came to Dido's death and the despairing cries of the dying queen, he broke down completely. "That will do, my boy, I'm tired," the doctor said tactfully, closing the book, and Hector rushed away "to vent my Virgilian grief in solitude."

Sent to Paris at eighteen to study medicine, he attended lectures long enough to become a bachelor of science, but he was seen at the opera house more often than in the anatomy theatre. The time was better spent in the library of the Paris Conservatoire, where he could memorize the scores of Gluck's operas. Within a year Berlioz's name was entered on the rolls of the Conservatoire, there to remain until he departed in 1830 with the first prize in composition.

It was while he was still a student that he discovered Shakespeare— "Shakespeare and Goethe! The mute witnesses of my torments, who have explained my whole life to me"—and simultaneously fell in love with the blonde Irish actress Harriet Smithson, who had come to Paris to play Juliet and Ophelia with Charles Kemble's touring company. The initial shock was almost more than he could bear:

"A Heart in Turmoil"

Harriet Smithson, shown below as Juliet in the clutches of Charles Kemble, was Berlioz's first love, and later, his first wife. Demure Miss Moke, a concert pianist, jilted him for a piano maker. In 1854 Berlioz married Marie Recio, his faithful companion for thirteen years and an aspiring but terrible soprano.

Camille Moke

Harriet Smithson

Marie Recio

"I could not sleep, I lost my spirits, my favorite studies became distasteful to me, I could not work, and I spent my time wandering aimlessly about Paris . . ." It was as totally unrequited as any passion could be; for several years he did not even succeed in being introduced to Miss Smithson. But out of this feckless experience was born the idea of a *Symphonie Fantastique* relating an equally anguished "episode in the life of an artist."

Berlioz's scenario for the symphony tells of a lovesick musician who takes a nearly fatal overdose of opium and sees his beloved, his *idée fixe,* in a series of feverish visions—at a crowded ball, in the solitude of the country, and (after he has been led to the scaffold for murdering her) at an orgy of demons on the witches' Sabbath. Most

of these ingredients will be familiar to readers of Mario Praz's *The Romantic Agony:* the intermingling of love and death, the attraction of the fatal woman, *la belle dame sans merci,* and the sadistic finale in the shadow of the divine marquis. Here, some of the central themes of romanticism are drawn together into a psychological web, at the center of which, like a giant spider, sits the artist's voracious ego, pursuing his quarry first in one direction, then another. The conception is utterly romantic, and yet the music has none of the murkiness of texture that one associates with other "confessional" symphonies of the nineteenth century. Berlioz's sound is lyrical and translucent, almost Mozartean, and even the explosive "March to the Scaffold"—a major breakthrough in percussion scoring, by the way—is structurally as classical as any march of Beethoven's.

The first performance of the *Fantastique*, on December 5, 1830, ushered in a new epoch for musicians, just as the première of Victor Hugo's *Hernani* nine months earlier had sounded the starting signal for a literary revolution. Franz Liszt, who was present at the concert (and afterward made a piano transcription of the *Fantastique*) tells us that this was a turning point in his life: "Those who watched the fires of genius consume the ancient, crumbling skeletons all attached themselves to that school of which Berlioz was the most gifted, audacious and brilliant representative."

By that time Berlioz had won the Conservatoire's Prix de Rome, a five-year fellowship that entailed two years of residence at the French Academy in Rome. He had dropped his stage-door passion for Miss Smithson in favor of a more promising courtship with a young pianist, Camille Moke, and when he left for Italy early in 1831, he considered himself engaged to be married. When the news came that she had jilted him for the piano manufacturer Pleyel, Berlioz came as close to committing suicide as the hero of his symphony. But though he felt "fierce as a chained dog" at the Villa Medici, the Italian spring quickly dispelled his misery. Armed only with his trusty guitar, he went hiking through the Campagna and the mountains of the Abruzzi, developing a taste for the roughest kind of folk music. What he liked best was "a leather-lunged peasant roaring out a love song under the window of his girl, to the accompaniment of a huge mandolin, a bagpipe and a little iron instrument like a triangle . . ." He was storing up enough scenic and sonic impressions to last a lifetime. Not only his next symphony, *Harold in Italy,* but all his dramatic works—with the exception of *Faust*— were henceforth to have a Mediterranean setting.

Back in Paris in 1832, he learned that Miss Smithson was now starring with her own company and piling up ruinous deficits at the box office. Returning to his original *idée fixe,* he sent her a ticket to his next orchestral concert. When the actress entered her box that evening, she may have been the only person in the audience who was unaware that she herself figured as the heroine of the program; all she knew was that the composer had once been in love with her. The *Fantastique* began the program. As Berlioz writes, "the passionate character of the work, its burning melodies, its cries of love, its accesses of fury, and the violent vibrations of such an orchestra heard close by, were bound to produce an impression." This is the comment of an aural erotic, a man in love with sound both for its own sake and for the effect it has on others. Harriet heard his violent vibrations and asked herself, "What if he loves me still?"

Next on the program came *Lélio ou la Retour à la Vie,* a sequel to the *Fantastique* that Berlioz had patched together from several miscellaneous choral and orchestral sketches. On stage they were linked together by an actor declaiming spoken monologues. When Harriet heard him apostrophize "Shakespeare, Shakespeare!" and call upon "this Juliet, this Ophelia whom my heart is ever seeking," she could no longer doubt what was happening. The room began going around in circles; she went home in a trance. The next day, Berlioz was formally introduced to her at last; it was December 10, 1832, and more than five years had elapsed since the night he had first seen her as Ophelia. They were married at the British embassy the following October, with Liszt as witness, but against the wishes of both families. He was not yet thirty; Harriet was thirty-three.

To pay her theatre debts and to provide for his growing family—a son, Louis, was born in 1834—Berlioz commenced his Augean labors as a critic. Even so, in the first years of his marriage he produced some of his finest

works. *Harold in Italy* reviews his Italian experiences—ostensibly the subject is Byron's *Childe Harold,* one of the "wanderers o'er Eternity"—and focuses on a kind of interior monologue. Nowhere in the whole orchestral repertoire is there a more subtle or breathtaking piece of music than the slow movement, where the melancholy solo viola is interwoven with the evening hymn of a passing pilgrim band. His next major score, the *Requiem,* demonstrates the power of massed voices and brasses as only Berlioz knew how to deploy them. His vision of the Last Judgment is spatially conceived: the main orchestra and chorus are surrounded by four satellite brass bands that answer one another over the heads of the audience in furious vectors of sound. This is an arrangement requiring split-second co-ordination, and Berlioz was never happier than on those rare occasions when he could conduct his preview of the Apocalypse:

The chorus sustained the assault of the orchestra without flinching; the fourfold peal of trumpets broke forth from the four corners of the stage, already vibrating with the rolling of the ten kettledrums and the tremolo of fifty bows; and in the midst of this cataclysm of sinister harmonies and noise from the other world the hundred and twenty voices hurled forth their terrible prediction . . .

The *Requiem* impressed the critics, but it could not make the walls of the Paris Opéra come tumbling down, and only by mounting a successful assault in that quarter could Berlioz hope to become self-supporting as a composer. Casting about for an operatic plot that would give him a chance to compete with Meyerbeer, he came up with a Renaissance autobiography that had recently been published in a new translation— the *Memoirs of Benvenuto Cellini Written by Himself.* Horace Walpole had pronounced it "more amusing than any novel I know." Berlioz, too, felt an instant affinity for the swashbuckling sculptor and set about recasting the book into a theatre mold.

Though the figure of Cellini dominates the proceedings, Berlioz also contrived to put the Roman populace onstage, in crowd and carnival scenes that anticipated *Die Meistersinger* and *Boris Godunov* by more than thirty years. Liszt says that in this brawling, turbulent score "the common people speak for the first time with their mighty and resounding voice." But it was the subscribers to the Opéra who had the last word. *Benvenuto Cellini* was "dragged to execution," as Berlioz put it, partly because it was sabotaged by a backstage cabal, and partly because it was too dazzling, too difficult, to fit into any of the established operatic categories. Even today, when everyone agrees that *Cellini* is a great opera, it is still the odd-man-out of the French repertoire.

The fiasco drove him back to the concert hall. Thanks to Paganini's princely gift of twenty thousand francs (equivalent to about $20,000 in modern terms), he was able to take time off from article-writing and concentrate his energies on the "sublime and ever-novel theme" of *Romeo and Juliet*. It was his first breathing spell in five years. "I worked seven months at my symphony, not leaving off more than three or four days out of every thirty on any pretense whatever. And during all that time, how ardently did I live!"

The result is a "dramatic symphony" in which the classicism of his sound and the romanticism of his subject are perfectly counterbalanced. It is a work of pure music, without scenery or costumes—an opera for the imagination, rather than a literal reconstruction of the play. Written for a generation that had rediscovered Shakespeare as the essence of romantic fantasy, it conveys mood and character by translating the story into a series of musical metaphors. "So you know nothing of *Romeo*?" Berlioz chaffed one of his friends. "I do ask you to sit down patiently and hatch out the adagio, and if sooner or later you don't see Shakespeare's two lovers come forth, if you don't see the moonlight shining through

the trees in Capulet's garden, if the duet sung by the violins and cellos, if the interminable farewells at the end, if all the palpitations, if all the embraces, if the devastating *forte* in E in double chords, do not wring your heart-strings, then the truth is you are a triple bound member of the Institute."

At home in Montmartre, meanwhile, Berlioz and the erstwhile Juliet were acting out the familiar tragicomedy of the aging wife and the handsome husband whose career puts him in easy reach of temptation. Harriet, grown plump and alcoholic, pursued her husband with a jealousy born of despair. At last he slipped off on a tour of Germany, where he thought his music would do better than in Paris, leaving a note on the mantelpiece. "But I did not go alone," he confesses sheepishly. "I had a traveling companion."

Marie Recio, his French-Spanish mistress, was a singer in her twenties whose figure was more admired than her voice. "She yowls like a cat," Berlioz once told the pianist Ferdinand Hiller in strict confidence. "That would not be altogether a misfortune if she had not the unhappy ambition to sing at all my concerts." To keep the peace, he was obliged to make a place for her on his programs. "And to sing what?" asks Legouvé maliciously. "To sing his music, his melodies! And he had to give way; he who was driven mad by one false note, who was made really ill by one false rhythm; he had to consent to hear his own works misrepresented, to conduct the very pieces in which he was being assassinated as a composer." Yet her other qualities were evidently more endearing, and after Harriet's death Marie became the second Madame Berlioz.

During his *voyages musicales* through Europe in the 1840's, Berlioz managed to put together most of his next major score, *La Damnation de Faust*. One episode was jotted down by gaslight in a Budapest shop, another occurred to him in Breslau, a third appeared to him in the night, in Prague. On a visit

to Rouen he wrote the love duet for Part II; much of the rest was sketched out at odd moments in Paris, "always improvised, either at my own house, or at the café, or in the Tuileries gardens, and even on a stone in the Boulevard du Temple." The best-known episode in the score, the "Rakoczy March," is an adaptation of a Hungarian folk tune that had caught his ear. Before conducting the first performance of this arrangement in Budapest, he was warned by a local editor not to begin softly, because "we are accustomed to hear it played fortissimo." Berlioz, sticking to his guns, insisted on starting piano and building up to a climax full of violent vibrations. "When, after a long crescendo, fugued fragments of the theme reappeared, interrupted by the dull beats of the big drum, simulating the effect of distant cannon, the room began to seethe with an indescribable sound, and when at length the orchestra burst into a furious melee, and hurled forth the long-delayed fortissimo, it was shaken by the most unheard-of cries and stampings; the concentrated fury of all this burning audience exploded in accents that made me shiver with terror."

Never one to waste a good effect, Berlioz grafted the march onto *La Damnation de Faust,* though it meant transporting Goethe's hero to Hungary as an excuse for having it there. Paris, unfortunately, was not as easily carried by storm as Budapest. On the day of the première, in 1846, the theatre was half-empty; most of the musical public had stayed at home, "caring as little about my new work as if I had been the most obscure student at the Conservatoire." He had paid for the performance out of his own pocket, and a second poorly attended concert left him still deeper in debt; the losses amounted to about ten thousand francs. He could face opposition, but not indifference, and this was the unkindest cut of all, for it robbed him of the will to go on composing. There is a tragic passage in the *Memoirs* where he describes an unwritten symphony in A minor, which he had heard in his dreams, with the first movement already fully scored, but which he had deliberately refrained from putting down on paper in order to save himself from still another cycle of disappointments.

"And now," he writes at fifty, "if not at the end of my career, I am at any rate on the last steep decline—exhausted, consumed, but ever ardent, and full of an energy that sometimes revolts with an almost overwhelming force. I begin to know French, to be able to write a page of music, or verse, or of prose fairly well; I can direct and inspire an orchestra; I adore and venerate art in all its forms . . . But I belong to a nation which has ceased to be interested in the nobler manifestations of intelligence, and whose only deity is the golden calf." In spite of a growing sense of futility, he went on producing masterpieces, though more sporadically than before. His Christmas oratorio, *The Childhood of Christ*, has a fragile archaic sound and tone colors that glow like a Romanesque madonna. The opera *Les Troyens* is an immense marble frieze by comparison—a full-scale setting of the Virgilian epic that had first aroused his imagination: the siege of Troy; Hector, Priam, Cassandra; Aeneas at Carthage with Queen Dido; the fateful cry of "Italie!" admonishing Aeneas that his destiny is to preside over the founding of the city of Rome; and Dido's soul-shattering suicide.

He spent three years on this "huge and therefore dangerous" project, writing both text and music. In the midst of it he was elected as one of the "Immortals" of the Institute, a distinction as welcome as it was overdue, for it brought him a yearly pension of fifteen hundred francs. The score grew steadily longer and finally had to be cut in half to make it stageworthy—*La Prise de Troie*, in three acts, and *Les Troyens à Carthage*, in five. When the work was done, he waited for someone to produce it. Instead there was a commission for an opera to inaugurate a

The moment of triumph, his first, came for Berlioz while on an 1867–68 tour of Russia. The photograph above, taken at that time, shows it came too late: the flamboyant composer has become an old man. Tired, subdued, critically ill, he died only a year later.

new theatre in Baden Baden, the fashionable watering place where he had conducted several seasons of summer concerts. The bandbox theatre was much too small for *Les Troyens*, but perfect for Mozartean opera, and Berlioz proceeded to write one—a sparkling, elegant comedy based on Shakespeare's *Much Ado about Nothing*. The music of *Béatrice et Bénédict* is illumined by the Italian sun and warmed by memories of bygone passions; one would think that only a young composer could have written such vibrant love duets. It struck him as ironic, after the 1862 première, that only now were people discovering "that I have melody, that I can be jubilant and even humorous." And yet, with *Béatrice* he took his last, mocking bow from the waist as a composer.

An abbreviated version of *Les Troyens* was produced at a Paris theatre in 1864 and ran for twenty-two performances. "Look, they are coming," a friend said to Berlioz one night as they watched the theatre filling up. "Yes, but I am going," was the laconic reply. Already he was suffering from a chronic stomach ailment that may have been cancer. Marie Recio had died of a heart attack in June, 1862; his son, a merchant-marine officer with a promising career, died of yellow fever in Havana five years later, at the age of thirty-three. "Absurdity now seems to me man's natural element," Berlioz wrote, "and death the noble goal of his mission." But Albert Camus writes of absurdity in *The Myth of Sisyphus* that there is no fate that cannot be surmounted by scorn.

Alone, without hopes or illusions, he undertook the concert tour to Moscow and St. Petersburg that was to be his farewell to music. Despite his illness and the strain of a long journey, the trip revived his spirits. Russia's young composers idolized him; in Moscow, with five hundred performers and a nearly delirious audience of twelve thousand, he made the deepest impression of his career. It was a clear-cut victory for the music of "passionate expression, inner fire, rhythmic drive and the element of surprise." And it gave the musical world its first inkling that Berlioz would one day emerge as "the fountainhead of modern music as Delacroix is of modern painting" (in Jacques Barzun's phrase).

After his return to France in the winter of 1868, his strength ebbed by degrees. On March 8, 1869, he died peacefully in the arms of Marie Recio's mother. Three days later he was buried with the pomp and ceremony befitting a member of the Institute and an officer of the Legion of Honor. Bizet, Gounod, Auber, and Thomas (whose music now sounds so old-fashioned compared to his) were among the mourners. As Berlioz had foreseen, one of the funeral orations was delivered by the same Conservatoire professor, Elwart, to whom he had once jokingly remarked, "If you're going to be at my funeral and make a speech, then I'd rather not die."

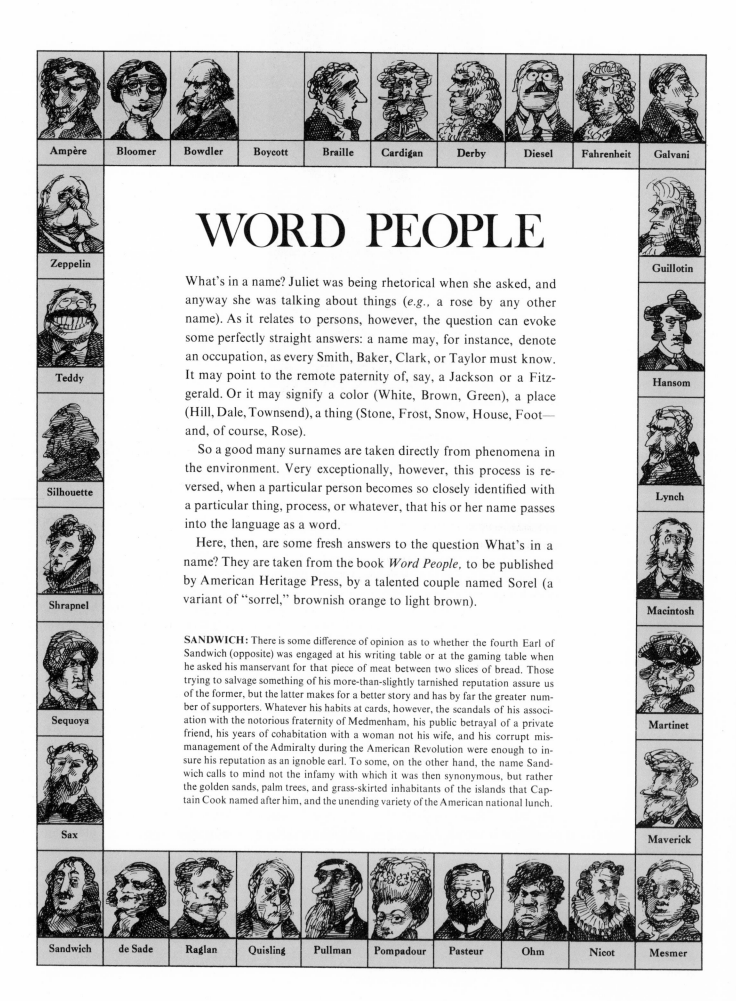

WORD PEOPLE

What's in a name? Juliet was being rhetorical when she asked, and anyway she was talking about things (*e.g.,* a rose by any other name). As it relates to persons, however, the question can evoke some perfectly straight answers: a name may, for instance, denote an occupation, as every Smith, Baker, Clark, or Taylor must know. It may point to the remote paternity of, say, a Jackson or a Fitzgerald. Or it may signify a color (White, Brown, Green), a place (Hill, Dale, Townsend), a thing (Stone, Frost, Snow, House, Foot—and, of course, Rose).

So a good many surnames are taken directly from phenomena in the environment. Very exceptionally, however, this process is reversed, when a particular person becomes so closely identified with a particular thing, process, or whatever, that his or her name passes into the language as a word.

Here, then, are some fresh answers to the question What's in a name? They are taken from the book *Word People,* to be published by American Heritage Press, by a talented couple named Sorel (a variant of "sorel," brownish orange to light brown).

SANDWICH: There is some difference of opinion as to whether the fourth Earl of Sandwich (opposite) was engaged at his writing table or at the gaming table when he asked his manservant for that piece of meat between two slices of bread. Those trying to salvage something of his more-than-slightly tarnished reputation assure us of the former, but the latter makes for a better story and has by far the greater number of supporters. Whatever his habits at cards, however, the scandals of his association with the notorious fraternity of Medmenham, his public betrayal of a private friend, his years of cohabitation with a woman not his wife, and his corrupt mismanagement of the Admiralty during the American Revolution were enough to insure his reputation as an ignoble earl. To some, on the other hand, the name Sandwich calls to mind not the infamy with which it was then synonymous, but rather the golden sands, palm trees, and grass-skirted inhabitants of the islands that Captain Cook named after him, and the unending variety of the American national lunch.

Ampère Bloomer Bowdler Boycott Braille Cardigan Derby Diesel Fahrenheit Galvani

Zeppelin Teddy Silhouette Shrapnel Sequoya Sax

Guillotin Hansom Lynch Macintosh Martinet Maverick

Sandwich de Sade Raglan Quisling Pullman Pompadour Pasteur Ohm Nicot Mesmer

DRAWINGS BY EDWARD SOREL   TEXT BY NANCY SOREL

GERRYMANDER: Elbridge Gerry had the best interests of the United States at heart, but he often found it hard to believe these best interests and his own personal views could be anything but identical. What is more, he seldom could say for certain just what his personal views were. He signed the Declaration of Independence, but not the Constitution, since it did not follow the lines he had proposed for it. He emerged from the "XYZ Affair" looking rather foolish, as he had convinced himself that he and he alone could prevent open war with France. Finally, in his second term as governor of Massachusetts, he turned all the Federalists out of office, right down to the local postmasters, attempted to have contempt of governor equated with contempt of court, and in a desperate effort to retrieve his lost prestige became party to the redrawing of Massachusetts voting districts into grotesque shapes to enable the Jeffersonians to retain their majority. "Why, it's a salamander!" one Federalist exclaimed, studying the tortuous, reptilian shape of an Essex county voting ditrict on a map. "No," another rejoined, "it's a gerry-mander!" In spite of his maneuvering, Gerry lost his own bid for re-election, but his party nominated him for vice-president; elected, he served under Madison until his death in 1814.

BLOOMER: Although she had persuaded her husband to omit the word "obey" from their marriage vows, Amelia Jenks Bloomer was no nineteenth-century Women's Liberationist. She would not sign the Declaration of Independence for Women that was drawn up right in her own town of Seneca Falls, New York, and her real concern was temperance, not feminism. But she rebelled at the voluminous hoop skirts that fashion decreed, which could hardly be propelled through a door and were ill-suited to the unpaved streets of small-town America. Still, even after she started *The Lily* (the magazine of the Seneca Falls Ladies' Temperance Society) and thus became editor of the first women's magazine in America, her neighbors were hardly prepared for her sudden appearance on the town's main thoroughfare with her skirt apparently shrunk all the way to her knees and the lower half of her legs enveloped in a kind of Turkish trouser. In truth, the credit for first wearing this scandalous attire must go to Elizabeth Smith Miller, daughter of the wealthy abolitionist Gerrit Smith. But Mrs. Bloomer had *The Lily*, which soon took up the crusade for dress reform, and the nationwide controversy that resulted became forever connected with her name. After Jenny Lind wore the new style in public, the furor became international. "I went yesterday . . . to see a group of Bloomers," wrote the Duke of Wellington to Lady Salisbury in 1851. "It is impossible that the Costume should be adopted." He proved right. The general mockery with which it had first been greeted never abated, and although the feminists continued to wear the bloomer for several years, in time they gave it up. Feeling herself a martyr in Seneca Falls, Amelia Bloomer and her husband moved west, where fame rather than ridicule had preceded her and where both she and her unconventional garb were duly and properly appreciated.

SIDEBURNS: When General Ambrose E. Burnside rode before his troops, a big, striking figure in undress uniform, fatigue cap, and large buckskin gauntlets, his guns swinging loosely at the hip, he looked the picture of the brave, dashing soldier. The great, bushy whiskers flanking his honest face were a kind of personal trademark; they went particularly well with his bluff, hearty manner and seemed to set him apart as somehow superb. In Washington, during the contagious excitement of the early months of the Civil War, the daily parade, at sunset, of his three-month volunteers became one of the sights of the town, and he commanded maneuvers before members of Congress and the Cabinet, Washington ladies, and occasionally Lincoln himself. Eventually he was persuaded to succeed McClellan in command of the Army of the Potomac, but after a single battle, the disastrous Union defeat at Fredericksburg, he was relieved. Much of the remainder of the war he spent in the West, where he had a prominent antiwar civilian arrested and tried before a military tribunal for "treasonable utterances" and then sent cavalry and infantry to Chicago to close down a newspaper that had dared to defend the victim. His gallantry, however—and his whiskers—were much admired by the belles of his generation, who would, no doubt, have been delighted by the manner in which his name is preserved in ours.

SILHOUETTE: Great was the rejoicing when, in 1757, Louis XV, prompted by his mistress, Madame de Pompadour, called on M. Etienne de Silhouette to rescue France from the financial morass in which she had sunk. The new controller general started out promisingly by pruning the pensions of the king's noble ministers, but when these palliatives proved insufficient, he resorted to moves that pointed up the treasury's impoverished state without doing much to mend matters, thereby damaging France's credit at home and abroad. He persuaded the king to order a large part of the royal plate melted down for coins, then announced sweeping new taxes; parliament balked, and Silhouette fell from public favor. He was forced out of office after just eight months, by which time his name had been affixed forever to the popular little shadow portraits that so aptly symbolized his shadowy, insubstantial financial policies.

POMPADOUR: Like M. de Silhouette, the king's mistress belonged to the bourgeoisie. For centuries the kings of France had chosen their mistresses from the nobility, and the nobles of France resented Madame de Pompadour as an upstart. She had won her position through wit, beauty, and cleverness, and she kept it by constantly exposing her royal lover to costly entertainments. At Versailles she lived in a profusion of mirrors reflecting the light of elaborate chandeliers hung from ceilings of painted Venuses—reflecting, too, her golden hair, dressed high back from the brow in the fashion that still bears her name. It was in her room that the king first received his new controller general. Silhouette came primed with figures, but the king only wanted to know whether the paneling in Silhouette's study was gilded. Poor Silhouette hadn't noticed; he stood dumb, and the king departed. "You should have answered something," Madame de Pompadour chided him. "He'd never have gone to check."

CARDIGAN: On April Fool's Day, 1854, the Earl of Cardigan, who was fifty-six and had never seen active service, was given command of the Light Brigade in Her Majesty's Expeditionary Force to the Crimea. He was delighted. For years he had been relentlessly drilling his regiment—the 11th Light Dragoons—to a perfection of precision and speed. He had long since equipped his men with their famous uniforms of cherry-colored trousers topped by jackets of royal blue edged with gold, furred pelisses, capes that glittered with gold lace, and high fur hats with brilliant plumes. The men were, he felt, supremely ready.

Once in the Criméa, however, the cavalry saw little action, and Lord Cardigan lost interest in his command. He left his men to the hardships of cold, bad food, vermin, and mud, and installed himself on his luxurious yacht in Balaklava harbor. When the Battle of Balaklava began, he joined his brigade in time to receive the famous ambiguous order from Lord Raglan, which was interpreted to mean that the Light Brigade was to charge the length of the North Valley straight at the main Russian battery.

Lord Cardigan's greatest redeeming quality was probably his dauntless courage. Seated stiffly erect on his favorite charger, looking quite splendid in his cherry and royal blue, he rode down the valley toward the white bank of smoke at the other end, and since he never looked back, he did not know that almost the entire Light Brigade fell behind him.

When, a month later, he gave up the war and returned to England, he was acclaimed the hero of the already legendary Charge of the Light Brigade. Crowds cheered him, the queen invited him to Windsor, and the woolen jacket that he had worn during the campaign was copied en masse, christened a "cardigan," and sold everywhere. But the men he had left behind to endure the terrible Crimean winter eventually came home, and the story of his indifference and neglect was revealed, to the considerable diminution of his glory.

CHAUVINISM: A French soldier of the Empire was Nicolas Chauvin. Little is known about him. He fought for Napoleon, was severely wounded and mutilated, and received as compensation and reward a saber of honor, a red ribbon, and a pension of two hundred francs, or forty dollars, per year. A modern soldier may not find this much to get excited about, but Nicolas Chauvin was not merely satisfied, he was extravagantly, almost deliriously, grateful. His enthusiasm for Napoleon was so great, and occupied so much of his conversation, that his comrades could not but ridicule him for it. Hence, we have chauvinism.

MESMERIZE: Dr. Franz Anton Mesmer was possessed all his life by the idea of an invisible magnetic fluid in which all bodies were immersed. He wore a magnet in a little leather sack around his neck and frequently experimented with it on inanimate objects; believing them capable of transmitting benef-icent powers through the surrounding fluid, he applied his magnet to cups and spoons, mirrors and bedcovers, even to his patients' bath water. Inevitably some people were cured, the news spread, and the magnet became the common panacea for gout and ear trouble, spasms and insomnia, paralysis and stomach ache. Not until he was famous, however, did Mesmer realize that the cure was not in the mag-net but in the stroking movement of his hand, his soothing voice, and his piercing gaze—all of which could, and often did, induce a hypnotic sleep in his patients. Exiled from Vienna, Mesmer became all the rage in Paris: Marie Antoinette found his treatment immensely beneficial, and the young Marquis de Lafayette, about to depart for America, wrote General Washington that he was bringing not only weapons but also *"le secret de Mesmer"*—for just what Revolutionary purpose history does not reveal.